Connecting with Your Kids

Fun, simple and practical ideas to help raise
resilient children

Andy McNeilly

A catalogue record for this book is available from the National Library of Australia

This book uses case studies to enforce the meaning behind its relevant chapter. Names have been omitted or changed to protect individual privacy.

Every effort has been made to trace (and seek permission for use of) the original source of material used within this book. Where the attempt has been unsuccessful, the publisher would be pleased to hear from the author/publisher to rectify any omission.

ISBN: 978-0-6484673-0-4

NATIONAL LIBRARY OF AUSTRALIA

A catalogue record for this book is available from the National Library of Australia

Contents

Foreword
Steve Biddulph

Have you noticed that some families seem to be like a happy party just walking along, and others are kind of tense and awkward? How some parents and kids seem to get along really well, and others are awkward and negative, reduced to just sharp commands to "hurry up" or "don't touch that".

It's not that one kind of parent doesn't love their kids just as much or work just as hard to feed and clothe and care for them, but more that they may not have found ways to be close, have fun, and share good times. Connection with our kids isn't some mystical thing, it's made up of shared activities and memories, often not the expensive ones but just stuff that happened.

Andy McNeilly realised early in his work as a primary teacher (and dad) that not all kids get along with their parents very well, and not all parents know what to do to have good times with their children. After all, what's the point of feeding, clothing and caring for kids if you still just don't get along, and they don't feel close to you and able to trust you. If they grow into teens, and then adults, who don't have much connection to you, and just drift away. How sad would that be?

The secret that Andy is happy to share is that there are thousands of things you can do with your kids, which are fun and helpful to building a good relationship. Don't be daunted by that, or by the pages of this book, into feeling that's just too much. This is a RECIPE book. Just one tasty "meal" from the activities in here can give you a really great time. Half a dozen of those might be all you need for a year!

And because our minds are good at knowing what works for us, just trust yourself to pick out one or two and make a start. You'll get your money's worth if even one of these ideas takes off with you and your children.

Sometimes as a parent, you feel stuck. Stuck for what to do, or what to say, or how to act. It's a terrible feeling, knowing there is something wise or clever or helpful needed, and you just don't know what that is.

These activities unstick you. You start to get more creative, and inventive, and get into a nice flow with your kids that spreads to other parts of your family's life. When I think back to my childhood sixty years ago (yes, shocking aye? And I look so YOUNG) I remember fun times with my mum or dad, doing stuff and feeling that the world and life were a wonderful place. Activities, conversations, projects, games, that are simple and may not even cost a cent.

Have fun with this book! Dive in somewhere, grab an idea, and give it a go.

Warmest

Steve Biddulph AM,
Author of 10 *Things Girls Need Most, Raising Girls, Raising Boys,*
Complete Secrets of Happy Children, and *The New Manhood*
www.stevebiddulph.com

Introduction

One of the best things I've ever done in my life was to have children. Daisy, Finn and Monty are special people in my life and I often marvel at the miracle of being a parent; being part of creating a child and helping them to grow, develop and become independent. When I find out that somebody is going to become a parent, I always tell them that this is the best thing they'll ever do in their lives.

I'm passionate about people being a part of a loving and connected family and there is nothing more satisfying for me than to work with people. I love connecting with people of all ages, from different backgrounds, countries and cultures, and from all walks of life. This has been a strong theme throughout my life. I have been teaching primary school-aged children for over a decade. I've also worked in adult education. But as a parent, I know how easy it is to get buried in the 'admin of life'.

We're all guilty of 'in a minute' syndrome: putting off being with our kids until we've sent that email, made that phone call or completed that task. But there is nothing more important than engaging with our kids. Developing this connection requires us to build a strong relationship with our kids so they know we are always there for them.

I want to share some insights I've gained from my many years as a primary school teacher and also my experiences as a parent. My aim is to give parents and kids the tools to connect and also for kids to make a success of their lives. This book is designed to give you the insights and practical strategies to make time to connect with your kids and to support them to build the life skills they need to thrive and be happy.

Happiness predicts success, not the other way around.

Our kids face numerous hurdles to happiness: the physical, psychological and social pressures of growing up in a changing world dominated by social media and the 'busyness' of their parents' lives. Most of us adults take our ability to cope with what life throws at us for granted. But that is an ability we've had to learn. We can support our kids to develop these 'executive skills' from a young age. The sooner we can equip our kids, the better. We have a critical role to play in helping our kids develop these skills, but we have to make time to do it.

More importantly, being connected as a family is one of the most special things that we can all experience in our lives.

We don't have to be a parenting expert, however we can always look at ways to become a better parent. I've written and designed this book to be simple and fun, and to be used together as a family. Each week, there are some fun activities to play with that are designed to build life skills. You might like to use this book in chronological order, or if you think that you would like to work on a particular life skill with one of your children, try finding the best skills that fit the needs of your family. The ideas in this book are often simple and easy for you to do with very few resources. They are designed to be fun and adaptable. Feel free to experiment and play with them, changing things around to suit your family. Some of the suggested ideas are very closely linked to the executive skill in each section and some are not. Many of them are linked to lots of other executive skills and quite a few have been repeated. And some of the stories are linked to the life skills, while some may have not much to do with them at all.

As Princess Diana said, "Family is the most important thing in the world."

Have fun playing with this book and enjoy connecting together as a family.

Cheers,

Andy McNeilly

Gratitude

> "He who knows he has enough is rich."
>
> Lao Tzu

Gratitude could be described as the quality of being thankful. Being grateful for something may help us to become connected with the present; not wishing for something from the future or not thinking about the past. There may be many benefits to us of being grateful, such as improved mental health, increased happiness and a reduction in depression. It seems to me that one of the quests of being a human being is to be happy. Sometimes, when I just stop and 'smell the roses', I become aware of how good my life really is.

I am so grateful for everything in my life, and for actually having a life to be grateful for. I went for a swim with our children Daisy, Finn and Monty. The wind was blowing and the seas were rough. We could have had a disastrous time at

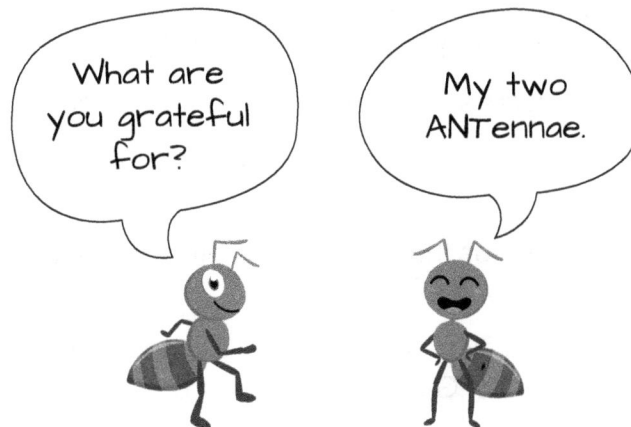

What are you grateful for?

My two ANTennae.

the beach, but we drove a short distance to a more secluded beach and had a wonderful time together. How grateful I was that we could go somewhere else. I felt grateful to have a car to transport us all in, to be able to park close to the beach and to be able to live in a place where our family is safe.

Sometimes, I dream of having more, but I am often reminded how grateful I am for what we already have. And I am truly grateful for my children. Simply stopping and considering what we do have, rather than wanting for more, helps us to simply appreciate things. We can feel more at peace and calm, which can be a wonderful experience. How lucky we all are to be alive.

Choose one idea from this list to try at home together as a family this week. Feel free to adapt or change it to suit your family. Maybe you have a different way to show gratitude as a family.

★ Write a letter or card to someone and thank them for something that they have done for you.

★ Name someone who has helped you become the person that you are today. Contact them and tell them.

★ Talk about all the things that you are grateful for in your lives.

★ Write a list of a dozen people in your life that you are grateful for. Share them with your family.

★ What's the best thing that has happened to you today so far? Discuss.

★ As a family, talk about what have you learned recently that will help you in the future.

★ What are the best things about your family? Make a list.

★ During dinner, discuss what worked well for you so far this week.

★ What made you smile and laugh today? Talk with the family about these things.

★ Make a list of 15 things that you are grateful for. Compare them with your family. Are any the same?

★ Think of someone who you are grateful to know and you have not contacted for a while. Give them a call or post them a card.

After listening to someone discuss the importance of gratitude one evening at Finn and Monty's school, the following night around the dinner table, I was talking with my family about gratitude; what it meant to me and how I thought it differed from luck. We all started to think about the things in our lives that we are grateful for. I shared how I was grateful for my family, my health, the job that I have and hours that I work, giving me so much family time, and the house we live in (it's not the best house around, but we all love it). Sandi, Daisy, Finn and Monty all shared many different things that they were grateful for; some I could have predicted, others surprising.

This was such a loving and caring mood that we created together. It was also such a different space to be in for me — I am often thinking of the next thing. What will I build next? What project will I take on? What toy will I buy next? I often forget to be present to what is 'now' and to appreciate what I truly am grateful for. This discussion around the table was such a wonderful experience for us where we all stopped and thought about all the things in our lives that are truly wonderful. It was such a precious conversation to share together.

> "Gratitude is the healthiest of all human emotions. The more you express gratitude for what you have, the more likely you will have even more to express gratitude for."
>
> Zig Ziglar

Empathy

> "Empathy is about standing in someone else's shoes, feeling with his or her heart, seeing with his or her eyes. Not only is empathy hard to outsource and automate, but it makes the world a better place."
>
> Daniel H. Pink

Some people may describe empathy as being the ability to feel what someone else is going through. We get to experience what someone else is experiencing. As they say, being able to put yourself into another person's shoes. Having the ability to be empathetic helps us to connect with others and build our relationship together. We may also find that more people want to be around us as our empathetic disposition helps us to relate with each other. Being empathetic can also bring us closer together, as others may feel they are heard and not judged.

Are you empathetic?

Sure, I can put myself into anyone else's shoes.

It may also help us to build trust in our relationships. When someone shows empathy towards us, we may feel that we are somehow experiencing the same emotions together. We can experience feeling 'together'; we are connected together, which can be a wonderful experience.

Following are some ideas to help you to connect and create empathy at the same time. Choose your favourite from this list and see what happens. Have fun!

★ Play a board game together as a family. Take note of everyone's emotions and how they change throughout the game. How do you think they were feeling?

★ Go for a walk to a local space, like the park or beach, and notice everything around you.

★ When you are down the street, from a distance, look at a stranger and wonder what their life is like. Discuss with the family when you get home.

★ During dinner, imagine what it would be like for some people who have very little to eat. How would they feel?

★ Can you imagine someone who would like some flowers that were picked from your garden? Why would they like them?

★ Next time you are at the shops, ask the person serving you, "What is something different that has happened to you today?" When you get home, talk about how you think that person would have felt.

★ Talk about who you think would benefit from a 'random act of kindness' and why they would.

★ Do you know someone who would really love a big hug from you? Discuss.

★ Who would get a surprise from receiving a letter or card from you? Why would that make a difference to them?

★ Do you know anyone who would love to have some of your clothes that you don't wear anymore? Discuss.

A while ago, I taught a bright young girl in Year Three. Her parents approached me about a concern this girl was having. She was counting everything and was worried that she was not normal. She sometimes would stress about her counting and work herself into a state of worry. I felt for this girl, that she was making a big deal about something that may occur to others as trivial. I could empathise with her; thinking that she was in some kind of way different to others, strange or even weird. I could imagine myself in her world of thinking that I was not normal, whatever that is.

Following this empathetic experience, I gathered the class together and I shared some of the weird things that I do, like counting the number of steps as I walk up a flight of stairs, or hanging a piece of clothing on the washing line with two pegs of the same colour. Other kids in the class shared how they do weird things too. As the discussion progressed, I saw this young girl come to the realisation that either she was as normal or as weird as everyone else, and she started to smile.

> **"**
>
> When we show empathy towards another, it can bring us closer together. "When you show deep empathy toward others, their defensive energy goes down, and positive energy replaces it. That's when you can get more creative in solving problems."
>
> Stephen Covey
>
> **"**

Creativity

> "Creativity involves breaking out of established patterns
> in order to look at things in a different way."
>
> Edward de Bono

I often hear people talking about others they know who are creative; artists, authors, chefs, hairdressers, photographers and the like. Some people may say that they themselves aren't very creative, however I'm not too sure. What about the stay-at-home parent who can manage the family, or the forklift driver who takes his family on a trip across the Simpson Desert in an old four-wheel drive, and the finance broker, who tends to an organic garden then makes a delicious meal for the extended family?

Creativity could be said to be using the imagination to make something. For some, creativity could be similar to innovation, imagination or originality. Other benefits of being creative could be managing conflict, the ability to be a team player or simply being able to solve problems.

I love being creative at home with the kids and will often build or make things with them in the garage. Monty and I made a billy cart from bits left from a building project, and Daisy and Finn helped him paint it. Monty made Finn a small stool that doubles as a storage box when turned upside down. Finn made a load of tea-light candles from some beautiful pieces of cypress pine for Christmas presents. Daisy painted colourful circles on the top of an outdoor table that was worn out and we were going to put out on the nature strip. We cut off the legs and it now hangs out the back on a fence as a piece of art. Sandi will come home from work and create an amazing meal from a fridge that looks empty to someone else. Being creative is something that we all are, even though we may be creative in so many different ways.

When we discover how creative we all really are, developing our creativity can be an extremely rewarding experience.

Being creative can be so much fun. Here are a few ideas to choose something from, to do this week with your family to foster creativity. Maybe you'd like to create a different idea?

★ Play 'Charades' by acting out words and syllables in the title of a movie, a song or a book.

★ Open a book and quickly point to a word without looking. Tell a one-minute story that includes your word.

★ Play 'Mr. Squiggle'. One person quickly draws a squiggle on a piece of paper and passes it along for the next person to complete the drawing.

★ Build something together with Lego, paper, playing cards, play doh or modelling clay.

★ Get out some pencils, crayons, paints and textas and work together to make something amazing.

★ Plan and prepare a family dinner party or picnic together.

★ Listen to some different radio stations and discuss the music.

★ Go for a walk in a local open space and look for traces of different animals that may live there. Talk about how these creatures are creative.

★ Rate your creativity skill on a level of 1 to 10. If you are below 10, discuss how you think you can learn to become more creative.

★ Cook something that you have never cooked before. Consider changing the recipe slightly. What did you discover? Discuss.

★ Around the dinner table, ask each other lots of crazy questions and take turns to answer them.

As our daughter Daisy grows older, I am continually surprised by her creativity. She plays the piano and guitar. She will paint, sew, cook, draw, construct with wood and even build with Lego. I am learning to cope with the mess she creates at the kitchen table or on the lounge room floor, often as dinner approaches, however her creativity is inspiring. Daisy will often sit for hours just being creative.

Recently, we built a small loft space for the kids and it is not uncommon to find it in a total mess (through my eyes) or as an inspiring city of Lego (as the children see it). As Daisy grew up, we gave her many opportunities to try different creative pursuits and now all of these opportunities are paying off.

When we discover how creative we all are, we can be in awe of ourselves and those around us.

> "Creativity is just connecting things. When you ask creative people how they did something, they feel a little guilty because they didn't really do it, they just saw something. It seemed obvious to them after a while. That's because they were able to connect experiences they've had and synthesize new things."
>
> Steve Jobs

Are you very creative?

Yes, I'm really talANTed.

Respecting Differences

> " "Strength lies in differences, not in similarities."
>
> Stephen Covey "

Every human being is different. We all look different, think differently and have different beliefs. Often, what you believe or what is important to you may have been taught to you from your elders or your peers, or you may have learned them from the environment you have grown up in. To respect other people for who they are and what they believe may help us to foster a more tolerant and caring community. It may create a more supporting and caring environment.

Some personal benefits of respecting the differences of others may be that we learn more about other cultures, and it could even help to create friendships with others who you may not have expected to. It might help us to be more empathetic or grateful.

I have travelled to many parts of the world and the best part of all the experiences has been all the people that I've met and the different cultures I have experienced. I've eaten in some amazing places and also had some terrible experiences in restaurants. Once, Sandi and I met a Vietnamese-American in Dalat, who invited us out. He kindly took us to a restaurant that had some local Vietnamese specialties. When the food arrived, to our surprise, each dish was filled with a different piece of offal, the most confronting was an eyeball soup, with eyes rolling in the light broth, looking at us, waiting to be eaten. That was a different meal, but I don't remember respecting it very much. However, I did enjoy that experience and have strong memories from it.

Respecting others' differences can lead us to many varied and sometimes rewarding life experiences.

Select your favourite idea from the following list to try together with your family this week. Change or adapt your choice to suit your needs.

★ Listen to music from a different culture. What was different compared to the music that you usually listen to?

★ Go to a religious event or ceremony and discuss what you noticed.

★ Find three facts about the indigenous people of your area and talk about what you discovered.

★ As a family, cook some food from a different culture that you haven't cooked before.

★ How are you different to others in your family? At school? Work? In your sports team? Discuss.

★ Go out to dinner to a restaurant from a culture that you have not experienced before.

★ Make a list together of all the rude and mean names you can call someone who is different to you. Which names do you think are terrible? Are there any that are not so bad? Talk about how those people might feel if you called them some of those names.

★ Watch a foreign film or television show together.

★ Meet with someone from a different culture and ask them about the country they came from.

★ Make a list of things you like and things that you don't like. Compare your list to other family members. What is different? Is there anything the same?

My family and I live in a beautiful seaside village in southern Victoria. Many people have made the 'sea change' and moved to this town from Melbourne in search of a different life to the ones they previously had in the city. It is a fairly monocultural town that you would expect to see on a postcard. On our first trip to Central Australia when the kids were young, we were wandering around Alice Springs when our son, Finn, saw an Indigenous Australian and asked, "Where is he from?" Years earlier, I remember standing in a queue at the airport in Bangkok when I heard a very strong New Zealand accent from behind me. I turned around and to my surprise, there was a young man of Asian origin standing there. I was expecting what I thought was a typical New Zealander — someone of European background. In my mind, I didn't even picture a Maori. Once making eye contact, I smiled at him and continued to wait in the line.

> "I look to a day when people will not be judged by the colour of their skin, but by the content of their character."
>
> Martin Luther King, Jr.

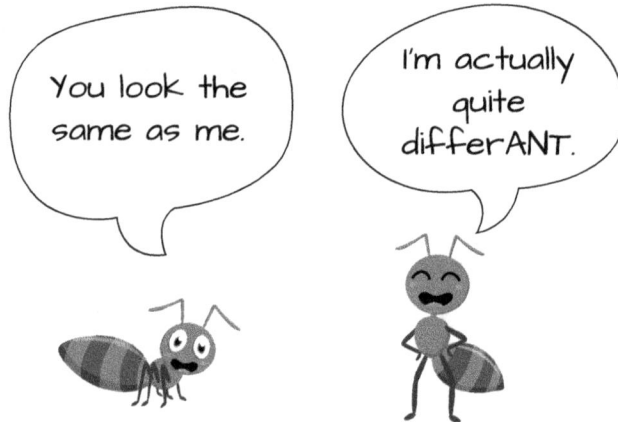

You look the same as me.

I'm actually quite differANT.

Staying Calm

> "Mistakes and pressure are inevitable; the secret
> to getting past them is to stay calm."
>
> Travis Bradberry.

Remaining calm when things start to get busy or stressful can be a wonderful skill to have. It may mean we appear not to be nervous, angry or to show any other strong emotions. Staying calm might be when we are able to take a breath, step back and evaluate the situation. By remaining calm and considering all the options when faced with challenges may actually enable us to save time and be more efficient. It may even help us to solve problems that others may find difficult when they become flustered or confused. Another benefit could be the ability to think clearly when placed under pressure.

There are two really great friends of mine, whom I love camping with. We met Tony and his family while on a trip around Australia and kept bumping into them in different places. They live in Central Victoria and we remain friends, often catching up. Clay is my other great friend, who loves camping. Clay and his family live close by and I had the pleasure of teaching one of his children in primary school. Tony and Clay are two of the calmest people I know. Tony works as a paramedic and Clay is a fireman. If there was an emergency, I cannot imagine any other two people I would rather have there in a time of crisis. They would remain calm and rational, and they would get the job done.

Choose something from this list to try together with your family to help you all learn to remain calm when placed in a tricky situation.

★ When you are feeling angry, how do you cool down and not blow your top? Share some strategies you use that might help you calm down when you are starting to feel this way.

★ Share what makes you mad then act it out when this happens to you. What did you notice? What did others notice? How did your body feel?

★ Take very deep and long breaths. What do you notice about your body? What about your mood?

★ Listen to some songs together. Which help you to relax and calm down. Are there some genres of music that do the opposite?

★ Play a board game or card game together. Notice your body and how it changes throughout the game. Talk about your body sensations when you have finished. Now try a different game and see if there are any different sensations that you experience.

★ Ask some of your friends or extended family how they remain calm when things get busy or they become stressed. Make a list of any ideas that you think you could use if you started to become stressed.

★ During the day, go outside and lie on the ground and look up at the clouds. What do you notice about your body? Listen to the sounds around you. Do any sounds make your body relax? What other sounds do you hear and what other sensations do you notice in your body?

★ Some people say that when they feel angry, they 'see red'. What colours describe other emotions? Which emotions would you prefer to feel when you are getting angry and what colour could they be? If you think you are starting to feel angry, what might happen if you think of a different colour? Discuss with your family.

★ Go for a walk together as a family. How does a walk make you feel? Could a walk help you if you were starting to feel upset? What other types of exercise might help you calm down? Discuss.

★ If you start to feel annoyed, what would happen to you if you made a fart noise? Are there any other noises you could create that would shift you from being annoyed to another emotion? Try making some different noises to each other and see what happens. What happens if you pull funny faces?

Working for years in hospitality gave me many opportunities to practise the skill of remaining calm. On a busy evening in restaurants, many people would come in and the orders would start to hit the kitchen. Sometimes stress levels would increase in the kitchen during service. There were many occasions where I would have disagreements with the head chef, Jeff; I was committed to getting the food to the table as quickly as possible and all meals going together. Jeff was committed to cooking and plating the best possible dishes that he could. Some of these disagreements became heated, but when I left the kitchen with a meal in my hand, I had to remain calm so the diner would experience a wonderful meal in a relaxed atmosphere. And, at the end of the night, Jeff and I would often have a laugh about some of our differences.

> "One important reason to stay calm is that calm parents hear more. Low-key, accepting parents are the ones whose children keep talking."
>
> Mary Pipher.

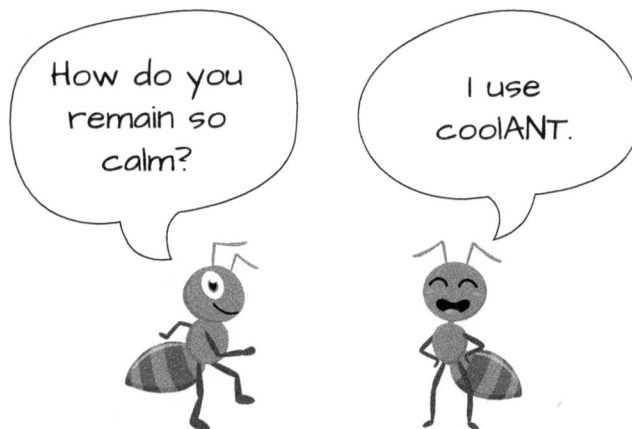

How do you remain so calm?

I use coolANT.

Growth Mindset

> " "There is a difference between not knowing and not knowing yet."
>
> Sheila Tobias

Growth mindset could be defined as one's ability to believe in themselves, to grow and develop through dedication and hard work. Some people may have had an experience or been told something in their past and then started to take this into their future. They may start to create a future that is determined by their past. For example, I remember from a young age that I was always good at maths, so I took this belief and made it fit my future. On the other hand, I remember believing that I was not a very good reader at school. I have a memory of reading with an older child in school, named Michael. From that day on, I believed that I was not good at reading. I took my past and made it my future.

However, with growth mindset, it is said that people can change this view. I can't remember consciously changing my view of my reading skill through dedication and hard work, but I now know that I'm not a bad reader, whatever that means anyway. Some say that adding the word 'yet' to the end of the sentence could change the whole meaning. For example, "I'm not very good at tennis," could create a future where there is little or no possibility of growth. "I'm not very good at tennis yet," may imply that improvement is not only possible, but probable in the future. Some benefits of practising growth mindset could be that we have an increase in self-esteem, particularly when learning something new. It may also help us to see setbacks or mistakes as a positive experience. Practising growth mindset could also help us to reduce stress levels as we may be less concerned about being perfect.

Here are a few things to try together to help foster a growth mindset. Choose one and give it a go this week, or change it to suit your family.

- ★ Discuss and reflect on what you learned today. What about this week?
- ★ What mistakes have you made lately? What did you learn from making those mistakes? Discuss.
- ★ Talk about what you haven't learned 'yet'.
- ★ What is a challenge that you plan to face this week? Discuss.
- ★ Discuss what you have been working hard on lately. How have you improved since you started?
- ★ What are you better at now than you were last year? What have you done to improve?
- ★ Some people say that the brain is like a muscle — the more you work your brain, the stronger it will be and the better it will perform. What do you think about this? Talk about how you might exercise your brain. What have you done lately to make yourself smarter?
- ★ Talk about what you are not perfect at. What are your imperfections? Are any of your imperfections similar to others in your family? Are your imperfections perfect imperfections?
- ★ Is there a time when you achieved something, but you didn't look for anyone's approval? Talk about times when you look for the approval of others.
- ★ What is failure? Talk about a time when you worked really hard at something, but did not achieve your final goal. What did you learn on your journey? What successes came out of your failure to achieve your goal?

I met my wife, Sandi, in London. At the time, she was working various jobs, earning enough money to get by. We cycled together around Europe, worked some more in London and then travelled back to Australia via the Trans-Siberian railway. When we returned, Sandi studied tourism. During her studies, she worked various jobs, including managing an arthouse cinema in Melbourne. As time went by, Sandi returned to study. This time, she undertook an Arts Degree, which she had always wanted to complete. We moved to Tasmania for some time, which interrupted her studies while she worked in tourism. We moved back to the mainland where Sandi continued her studies in Bendigo before gaining her degree with honours. She also graduated with a teaching degree. After doing some part-time relief teaching, Sandi gained employment working in various libraries around Geelong. Once again, Sandi returned to study — this time a Master's Degree in Information Services, which would give her professional qualifications as a librarian. Sandi currently works as a Children's and Youth Librarian at one of the branches in Geelong. I can't imagine the day when Sandi is not learning.

> "What can I learn from this? What will I do next time I'm in this situation?"
>
> Carol Dweck

Why do you have a growth mindset?

Because I value effort over talANT.

February Week 3

Self-Awareness

> "To realize that you do not understand is a virtue; not to realize that you do not understand is a defect."
>
> Lao Tzu

Self-awareness may be defined as being aware of one's own feelings and qualities. It may be knowing who we are so that we can understand how others see us. Being self-aware could be a useful skill for us when working or interacting with others. I would say that I am passionate about many things and often during discussions, I have been carried away. I have found that often, I've become excited and have forgotten to listen to others. By becoming aware of this, I often now catch myself out and find that I interrupt others less. Being self-aware can help us to know what to do and to know what not to do.

Do you notice how attractive I am?

Yes, you're very elegANT.

Following is a list of some ideas that may be useful to your family to help teach self-awareness. Have the youngest member of the family choose one to try this week.

★ Give a one-minute talk without any planning about all the good things about you.

★ Have a 'friendship' discussion. What makes a good friend? Why are you a good friend? Who are your good friends? What makes them a good friend to you?

★ What do you really like to do in your spare time? Talk about why you think you like to do those things.

★ Is there anything that you avoid doing? Why do you think this is so? Discuss.

★ Write a list of all your strengths and your weaknesses. Talk about them with others in the family.

★ Talk about what makes you happy/sad/angry/frustrated/ecstatic, etc. If you are feeling an emotion that you don't like, can you change it?

★ Notice how you are feeling right now. Notice how your body feels. How are your shoulders? Your jaw? Your back? Your stomach? Your posture? Notice what happens if you change your posture? What happens if you stand up? Lie down? Roll into a ball?

★ Download a meditation app and use it to help you meditate. What did you notice about yourself? Try meditating a few times during the week. Discuss if you noticed any changes each time you meditated.

★ How do you think other people perceive you? What do you think they would say are your good and not so good characteristics?

★ Write down five strengths that you think you have. Then interview someone else and ask them to list five strengths that they think you have. Compare the lists.

When mobile phones first came out, I could never understand why people became so attached to them. When I eventually purchased my first mobile, I shared it with my wife, Sandi. More often than not, she would take it. I wasn't really interested. As time passed, I eventually bought my own mobile and later on, a smart phone. I started to become more and more reliant on my device, taking it everywhere and always using it. I think that smart phones are amazing. There is so much that I can do on it and so many of the apps are brilliant. Lately, I've noticed that I have been using it way too much and becoming distracted when around others. I'll be checking emails and answering texts. I'll check the footy score or the weather. So, recently, I've started to change things. I've taken many of the apps off my phone that I have been distracted by and will instead, look on my computer when I'm home. For me, the thing that is different with the laptop is that I have to go and open it, whereas my mobile is usually in my pocket. I have also started unsubscribing to many emails. And I am starting to leave the phone at home when going out with the family. I'm also taking it out of my pocket and leaving it at the other end of the house when I'm home with the family.

> "Your visions will become clear only when you can look into your own heart. Who looks outside, dreams; who looks inside, awakes."
>
> C.G. Jung

Resilience

> "Persistence and resilience only come from having been given the chance to work through difficult problems."
>
> Gever Tulley

During our lives, we will all often experience times when things become challenging or difficult. It can be said that many of these experiences help us to grow. However, some of these times can prove to be more difficult than others. It's during these times that being resilient can help us to recover and push through. Being resilient is the ability for us to recover quickly or bounce back from difficulties we may experience. If you know a friend who is resilient, you may notice that they seem to be more positive than others or may appear to be more optimistic.

Recently, my mum had a fall while she was doing some gardening. At first, she found out that she had broken a few bones in her wrist and a couple of bones in her hip. It was later discovered that she had also broken some bones in her spine. Although her recovery was slower than she would have liked, Mum was able to push through the tough times. She organised to stay with different friends during her recovery before eventually moving back home.

Some other benefits of being resilient could include remaining focused on a task when faced with challenges or setbacks. It may also help us to understand that struggles in life can help us to grow, rather than looking at them and thinking "Why me?"

Try one of these together this week with the family to help build resilience.

★ Name something bad that happened to you in your past and then say something good that happened from of it.

★ What have you learned in your life by taking risks and making mistakes? How did you keep going when the going got tough?

★ Create and act out a short play about a time when someone failed at something or found the going tough. In the play, show how the character bounced back from the challenging situation.

★ Think about a time when the going was tough. After a few minutes of thinking about that time, notice how your body is. Now, stand up tall and lift your shoulders. Take a few deep breaths. What do you notice?

★ Discuss challenges in your life that you have found difficult and how you overcame these challenges.

★ Play a board game or card game together. When finished, talk about how it felt to win or how losing made you feel.

★ Go on a long walk together where you are all pushed out of your comfort zones.

★ Talk about the different areas in your life that you are resilient. Are there any areas that you are not so resilient? Why do you think this is? How could you change this?

★ How important is winning to you? Talk about things that are really important to win and other things that don't really matter. Why do you feel differently about these different activities? How do you feel when you don't win?

★ When you are feeling a little unhappy or a bit down, sit around and tell each other jokes or talk about funny things that have happened to you. What do you notice?

Many years ago, I knew a builder called Tim. He did this for many years until he decided on a career change. Tim studied and worked hard before eventually earning his helicopter licence. After flying for some time, Tim had an accident in his helicopter, which ended his new career and changed his life forever. The doctors told him that he would never walk again. After a lot of hard work, Tim managed to regain the use of his legs. He also decided on another career change; this time Tim went back to university to study architecture. I haven't seen Tim for a long time, but the last I heard, he had graduated and is now working as an architect. Can you imagine a better person qualified to design your building than someone who understands building construction and can make it accessible for all?

> "Nobody can hurt me without my permission."
> Mahatma Gandhi

Forming Relationships

> "The meeting of two personalities is like the contact of two chemical substances: if there is any reaction, both are transformed."
>
> Carl Jung

I looked up many definitions for the word 'relationship' regarding human beings, and the one common thread was 'connection'. There were three main connections defined; through blood, through marriage or an emotional connection between people. But are these the only connections we have in a relationship? When first born, babies start to form relationships with their parents immediately. As they grow, they form relationships with other family members and people in the community. This seems to be a very natural part of being a human. So, why would this be such an important skill to develop further? Some would argue that this skill is vital for us to thrive in the various communities that we all live in. Many employers are looking for people who are skilled in this area.

Ever since I was a teenager, I've always had a job when I wanted one. I worked delivering newspapers, helping the milkman, working in a pharmacy making deliveries on my bike and cleaning up in a butcher's shop. As I grew older, I started to work in restaurants where I developed my love of food and working with people. I believe that I have been able to get these jobs by building relationships with a wide range of different people.

Another benefit of being able to form relationships with others could be that we may be able to collaborate more effectively. It may also help us to simply enjoy being around others.

This week, choose one of the following to try together with the family. Feel free to adjust one of them to make it more suitable for your family.

★ Ask someone what they are really passionate about and listen to what they have to say without interrupting them.

★ Phone a friend or relative and discuss a fond memory you have about them.

★ Go for a walk down the street. Every time you pass someone, make eye contact and give them a smile.

★ Do something extra by helping at home without being asked.

★ Organise a picnic and invite other families along.

★ Write a card to someone and tell them something that you really like about them.

★ Tell someone that you love them and give them a really big hug.

★ Next time you are at school or work, talk to someone who you don't normally talk to.

★ Organise a board game or card game afternoon with some friends.

★ Go for a walk or bike ride with a friend or family member.

For me, forming relationships with other human beings is what I really love to do. For most of my working life, I have worked with people. I love working with others and I like to be of service to them, helping in any way that I can. My wife, Sandi, knows that I like to spend time with others. Before we had children, when we were out with friends or at a party, she would tell me she was ready to leave. We both had an unspoken mutual understanding that this was about a one-hour warning. As usual, the hour passed with me talking to anyone who would listen. I was always surprised when she came up and told me she was ready. Where did that last hour go? Things changed when we had our daughter, Daisy. The unspoken 'one-hour warning' completely disappeared. Sandi wouldn't tell me that she was ready to leave, it was replaced with "Let's go!" Either Daisy was crying or hungry (or both), or we had to get home to Daisy if she was there with grandparents. I'm not really sure if this story is all about forming relationships, but sometimes a story helps us to connect and form relationships together.

> "When dealing with people, remember you are not dealing with creatures of logic, but creatures of emotion."
>
> Dale Carnegie.

Patience

> " "Nature does not hurry, yet everything is accomplished."
>
> Lao Tsu "

Patience may be defined as the ability to accept delays without becoming annoyed, and remaining calm. It may help us to persevere with something when we experience difficulties, to continue without complaining.

I have noticed that patient people tend to be calmer and more relaxed. They may arrive somewhere a few minutes later than someone who raced to be on time, however they tend to arrive in a calmer state of mind. Perhaps these people may be present more quickly once they do arrive, whereas the person who arrived on time after rushing might take a while to calm down?

Hurry up or we'll be late.

Just be patiANT.

When we are patient, we tend to be able to problem solve in a calmer and more methodical manner. We may take our time to think of different solutions to problems or challenges we face. As they say, 'patience is a virtue'. Some of the following ideas might help to teach patience. Choose one to try together this week together.

- ★ Play a board or card game with the family.

- ★ Sit in the lounge and read together.

- ★ After dinner, see how long you can sit still in silence without communicating with anyone. The person who lasts the longest is the winner.

- ★ Have a discussion with the family in silence by writing down what you want to say. You can only use one piece of paper and one pencil.

- ★ Everyone draws a crazy scribble on a blank piece of paper. Pass it to someone else and have them carefully colour in each part of the scribble.

- ★ Get an egg and see how long it takes you to balance it on the table standing on its end.

- ★ Build a house of cards. How high can you build it?

- ★ Sit around together and quietly start to breathe deeply together. Close your eyes and notice your breathing. As you begin to relax, see if you can breathe more deeply. See how long you can continue to breathe deeply with your eyes closed. What did you notice?

- ★ Get a texta and scribble onto a blank piece of paper then colour each enclosed space with a coloured pencil.

- ★ Talk about all the things where patience is an absolute must. Are there any situations where you find yourself becoming impatient?

I love to build things using recycled materials. I've made a gate from a recycled roof structure, screen fences from old hardwood fence palings, a stand-up table with a hardwood top and Monty and I made a kennel for our dog, Rufus, using left-over plywood from our house renovation. Quite often, I'll have a design in mind then I'll sketch out the plans before starting construction. I will head off to the hardware store and purchase the timber for the frame. When home, I'll cut up the timber and put it all together. The next step is to find the recycled timber. More often than not, I won't have any recycled hardwood yet. So, when cycling to work, I'll start to ride, taking different routes. It may take a little longer for the commute, but I'll start to look out for unwanted hardwood. This will often take a few weeks trying to source the best materials to complete the project. I won't compromise and use an old fence that was made of treated pine. I keep searching for the right timber to complete the project. So far, my patience has paid off and each job has the particular worn and loved look I've been after.

> "The two most powerful warriors are patience and time."
>
> Leo Tolstoy

Making Requests

> "Making a request is much more powerful than asking a favour."
>
> Andy McNeilly

Making a request in its simplest form is just asking someone for something. However, the person asking someone to do something may be waiting for a long time for their request to be fulfilled if the request doesn't have a 'by when' attached to it. For example, "I request you finish this task by Thursday," would more likely gain a result when the result is needed.

What can be more fun is to make an 'unreasonable request' of someone. What you determine is unreasonable is up to you. The person receiving the request has three options: Firstly, they can decline to carry out the request. Secondly, they can accept. And, finally, they can make a counteroffer, or change the request. Once I became clear about the difference between making a request and asking a favour of somebody, I discovered that it was more powerful to make a request. For me, asking a favour of someone is linked to helping out, being kind or being nice. A request, on the other hand, is simple. Someone can accept the request, decline or make a counteroffer. Making a request can help us to be clear with each other about what is being asked and when it is requested to be done by. It can help us all to avoid disappointment.

I request that this week you try one of the following ideas together as a family.

★ Make three requests of someone in your family in one go. The person must first listen to all three requests before choosing one to accept, declining another, and making a counteroffer for the third one.

★ Think about a request that you could ask of someone in your family that you would almost certainly guarantee they would accept. Their job is to decline. Your job is keep making the same request and their job is to continually decline. What did you both notice?

★ Write down a list of requests to make of different people in your family. Your task is to predict if each request will be accepted, declined or counteroffered.

★ Make a list of all the jobs that are done around the house each week. Each person gets to choose one of the jobs from the list and request that someone else does that task. What happened?

★ Think about your favourite game and request that others play that game with you.

★ Make a request of someone that they cook your favourite meal. Did they accept, counteroffer or decline your request.

★ Create some blank cards with 'accept' written on some and 'decline' written on others. Cards are placed face down on the table. Take it in turns to make requests of someone before they draw a card to see if they accept or decline your request. Should they need to complete the task if they turn an 'accept' card? Consider adding a 'counteroffer' card into the game.

★ Choose a family movie and request that others in your family watch it with you.

★ Have someone make a request of you. Your job is not to accept or decline the request, but to make a counteroffer of their request. Did they accept or decline your counteroffer?

★ Make a list together of some unreasonable requests that you could make of others. Discuss why you think they are unreasonable requests. Pick a few unreasonable requests from your list and try them on some of your friends or family. What did you notice?

When I started teaching, I became involved with helping to run the annual school fair. After a couple of years, I was coordinating the whole event. The fair was the major fundraiser for the school, bringing in extra money to run programs and provide facilities for the children. The event was always scheduled for early on in the year when the weather is usually predicted to be fine.

The start of any school year for a teacher is always hectic; setting up the classroom, establishing relationships with new students and sorting out all the administrational paperwork. Running the school's fair at that time of the year would be nearly impossible to do on my own. As the coordinator of the fair, I needed to make requests of parents and teachers within the school community. Many people volunteered their time, however there were still so many tasks that needed to be completed. Making requests of others was the only way to get the job done.

> "Unfettered access is an unreasonable request."
>
> Jack Finn

Teamwork and Collaboration

> **“** If you want to go fast, go alone. If you want to go far, take others with you.”
>
> Native American Indian saying **”**

Teamwork or collaboration, what's the difference? Some people may say that teamwork is when individuals work in isolation to achieve a team goal whereas collaboration is working together to achieve a goal. There may be other differences. Teamwork could be the combined effort of a group creating efficiency in achieving an outcome. Collaboration could be seen as the combined effort of more than one individual to produce something. But, does it all really matter? I really enjoy working with others; some things I love to do and others I find myself avoiding. I don't enjoy reading large slabs of legal texts. And I'm not a fan of spending time researching stuff that I find boring, either in books or on the internet. Balancing financial budgets isn't really my thing either. However, I enjoy being creative and spending time with people. So, when I'm collaborating with others, I like to find people who enjoy doing things that I don't and hopefully I'll be doing things that they'd prefer not to do.

When organising a bike ride from Sydney to Barwon Heads, Mikey took care of the route. Lawrie organised accommodation. Simon and Nev organised team uniforms. I organised food and sleeping arrangements. Everyone else did their part and the whole ride went without incident.

Collaboration can help us to spread the tasks to ensure not only that everything gets done, but everyone can contribute to an end product. It can also help us to build relationships with others when working together.

As a family team, choose one of the following to do this week together.

★ Stand next to each other with your hands beside you. At the same time, everyone reaches in to the middle and holds hands. Together, you need to untangle the knot of hands without breaking the chain. The idea is to finish in a linked circle.

★ Using only a newspaper and sticky tape, work together to build the tallest construction you can.

★ Blindfold one member of the family. Set up an obstacle course with furniture and work together to guide the blindfolded person around the house only using words.

★ Grab an orange and hold it under your chin without using any hands. Stand in a line and pass the orange from one person to the next. Try the same except use a balloon between your legs.

★ Plan a family trivia night where you invite two or three other families over to play against each other.

★ Make a circle with a piece of rope. Have everyone stand in the area without anyone falling out. Now make the circle smaller and try again. How small can you make the circle before it is too small?

★ Make a house of cards together as a family. How can you make sure that everyone contributes?

★ Play a board game or card game that requires you to work in teams.

★ Plan and cook a family meal or picnic together where everyone must contribute. Remember, this includes shopping and cleaning up when you have finished.

★ Find an area in your house where it needs a tidy up or clean. Plan who will do what tasks to ensure the job gets done efficiently.

One thing I love to do is work around the house. I love small projects and sometimes I'll take on a larger project. After a renovation where the old garage was converted into a studio space, the outdoor area at the back of the new studio was uninspiring. We decided to make a deck to utilise the space that was once unused. I set to work to build the frame with some help from a carpenter friend, Gavin. We got most of it done in a couple of days. A good friend, Andrew, came over the next day and helped sort, cut and nail the boards into place. My kids, Daisy, Finn and Monty, all grabbed a hammer and started to nail in the deck boards after I drilled the holes. Even Andrew's son, Daniel, helped. With a lot of persistence, effort and loads of teamwork, the deck was completed within a week. The deck looks great and is often used in the afternoon to sit on and chat as the afternoon sun starts to disappear.

> "Talent wins games, but teamwork and intelligence wins championships."
>
> Michael Jordan

Individually, we are great.

But as a team we're fANTastic.

April Week 1

Critical Thinking

> "Economists who have studied the relationship between education and economic growth confirm what common sense suggests: The number of college degrees is not nearly as important as how well students develop cognitive skills, such as critical thinking and problem-solving ability."
>
> Derek Bok

Critical thinking could be defined as the process of gathering information and analysing it to solve a problem. It may require us to use a range of other executive skills rather than simple memorisation and recall of facts. Critical thinking allows us to objectively examine information to help make a judgement.

I remember working with my friend, Jeff, many years ago (before Google) to help him cut the rafters (the sloping beams that help to support the roof) of a cubby house he was building for his kids. Getting the cuts in the correct place turned out to be trickier than we first thought, being the non-builders that we were. We measured them and made the cuts, but they didn't fit correctly. So, we tried again and the second cuts didn't fit either; however, we didn't give up. We looked carefully at the problem and went back to the drawing board. Eventually, we managed to work out where the cuts went so the rafters fitted neatly onto the walls. The cubby house is still standing; however, it is now a magnificent chook pen.

Critical thinking could help us to promote creativity when problem solving and may help us to self-reflect. Some people believe that it also helps us to enhance our academic performance.

Choose one of the following to try this week to help enhance your critical thinking skills.

★ Give the answer first and then everyone needs to make questions that will give the chosen answer; e.g., the answer is butter. What are the questions?

★ Make some 'brain teasers' to challenge each other with, e.g., PROM ISE = broken promise, or EVER EVER EVER EVER = forever.

★ Play 'Two Truths and a Lie'. Someone says three things about themselves and everyone must guess which is the lie.

★ Find a conundrum book or Google 'conundrums' and share them with your family.

★ Think of a challenge you faced recently. List five different ways to overcome that challenge if you were to face it again.

★ Play 'Celebrity Heads' or 'Guess Who' with the family.

★ What if the sky was red? What if humans did not have a mouth? What if we lived on Mars? What if dogs could talk? Discuss these and then make some more of your own.

★ Talk about some facts that you know. How do you know that they are facts? Could these facts be wrong? Could they be opinions? Discuss.

★ Get some pictures from a newspaper, or Google some random images. Discuss what could be happening in each picture?

★ Find a range of items from around the house. Talk about what each item is used for. Now discuss what else it could be used for. How many different ideas can you come up with for each item?

To this day, many years after finishing Grade Six at primary school, I still have fond memories of my teacher, Mr. Ransom, who made learning fun. Grade Six was filled with games, creativity, brain teasers and conundrums. A few favourites come to mind. The first one went something like this... An electric train was travelling in a southerly direction at a speed of 50 km/h. It was going into a headwind that was blowing directly towards the train from the south at a speed of 50 km/h. Which way did the smoke from the train go?

The other conundrum that I can still remember was about the rooster sitting on the top of a house. It was sitting exactly in the middle of a pitched roof that came to a sharp point. It lay an egg which softly landed right on the point of the roof. Did the egg balance on the top of the roof or did it roll off, and if it did, which way did it roll; towards the front garden or towards the back garden? I still love the challenge of solving these types of conundrums and I really enjoy working with others to solve them.

> "Coming up with a way to fix mistakes challenges your creativity and your critical thinking skills and your resourcefulness. Often, you end up with something better than what you planned on in the first place."
>
> Mark Frauenfelder

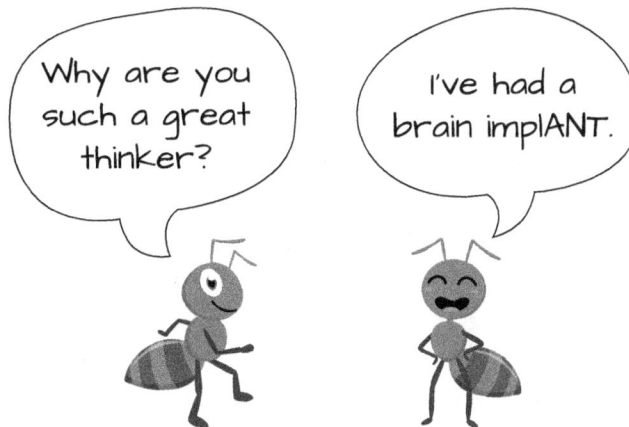

April Week 2

Decision Making

> "Good household decision-making often relies on thinking about your household like a firm."
>
> Emily Oster

Think quick — make a choice now! We have all been in this situation many times before. When we are competent with something, like riding a bike, making a split-second decision can come naturally to us. However, when we are learning something new, or have not yet mastered a task or activity, making decisions may not come so quickly. It may require more thought and analysis of the situation. Decision making could be thought of as the process of evaluating the alternatives and choosing the best option.

When riding my bicycle, I am able to quickly take all my past experiences and knowledge to safely escape tricky situations, well so far. It happens so quickly and effortlessly that it may appear to the observer that I was just lucky, like the time I was riding along in the dark and a rabbit crossed my path. It was either me or the rabbit and it came out second best, while I managed to stay on two wheels. On the other hand, I remember sailing in Oyster Bay in the east coast of Tasmania on a catamaran on a windy day. Being an inexperienced sailor, a wind gust blew and I was too slow to make a decision so the boat capsized. Benefits of being able to make a decision quickly might help us to save our time and energy.

Saying all this, sometimes decisions may not need always to be made too quickly. Standing back and looking at all the facts can be critical to help us to decide the best course of action.

Study this list together and quickly decide which one you would like to try this week together.

★ Each person gets two different items. Take it in turns to put the first two items on the table. Everyone must choose one item and point to it as quickly as they can. Discuss why you chose that item.

★ Think about two meals you are planning to cook during the week. Tell everyone what these meals are and the person who makes the fastest choice, decides on that meal the next day.

★ Give someone two different characters to role play. They must choose one quickly then act out that character for one minute.

★ Read a picture storybook together. Choose which character is your favourite and discuss why.

★ Someone says two different colours. The person sitting next to them must quickly choose a colour and say why it is better than the other colour. Repeat this game but change colours to animals, cities, toys, etc.

★ Get out two different board games. Have one person quickly choose which game to play together.

★ Read two picture storybooks and quickly decide which one is the best. Discuss why you chose that book.

★ Go for a bike ride or walk together. Each time you come to a junction, flip a coin to decide which way to go. See where you end up.

★ Play a board game in pairs and each time it is your turn, work out what to do between the two of you.

★ Next time you are getting dressed on the weekend, let someone else choose what you are to wear.

During my years at high school, I was always working. I delivered papers, helped the local milkman, worked at the petrol station and also in the butcher shop.

Eventually, the butchers took on an apprentice, so they had no need for me anymore. This sent me off looking for another job. I eventually found a restaurant in a trendy area of Melbourne where I started bussing tables, which involved clearing plates, cleaning tables and setting them up for the next customers. This was my first job in hospitality. Nearly 20 years later, I was working at a resort on the east coast of Tasmania when I decided that it was time for a change. Without any thought or idea of what was ahead, I chose to go back to study to become a primary school teacher. Over a decade later, I am clear that this was the right decision for me.

> "Inability to make decisions is one of the principal reasons executives fail. Deficiency in decision making ranks much higher than lack of specific knowledge or technical know-how as an indicator of leadership failure."
>
> John C. Maxwell

April Week 3

Written Communication

> "To effectively communicate, we must realize that we are all different in the way we perceive the world and use this understanding as a guide to our communication with others."
>
> Tony Robbins.

I've been inspiring children to write and teaching them these skills for many years. One of the greatest experiences teaching young children to write is to watch their skills grow so quickly. At the start of Year One, when the children are aged around five, I will often give them many opportunities to write. It is wonderful watching them learn to form the symbols on paper that will enable them to communicate. As they attempt to write, I will often ponder in amazement that human beings have created such an amazing method of communication; a collection of small circles and lines connected to make words.

Once completed, the children will buzz with amazement at what they have created and run up to show me their writing. They are beaming with pride and it brings a smile to my face. I will take their book and congratulate them on their efforts while looking at the creative scribbles that are sometimes off the lines. Often, I won't be able to read their writing, so I will ask them to read it back to me. Some children will remember what their scribbles were meant to say. Others will bumble through and make some of it up, while a few will say, "I've forgotten what I wrote." Toward the end of the year, I'll sit with each child and we'll compare their writing from the start of the year to where they have progressed, while we both marvel at their growth. It is so humbling to be at the start of these human beings' written communication journey and to see them begin to discover the power of words. Written communication can be advantageous to us as it provides a permanent record for future reference. Another benefit is that it may provide us with time to compose what exactly it is that we want to say; we can be extremely clear by drafting and redrafting our communication.

Have fun choosing one of the following to try together to help foster the skills of written communication.

★ Get some scrap paper and write some short text messages or emails that may have more than one meaning.

★ Write out some simple instructions for someone to follow. Give them to a partner and see what happens. Did they do what you wanted them to do?

★ Write a letter or postcard and mail it to a friend or family member. Even consider making your own postcard by writing your message on the back of a photo.

★ Leave some notes hidden around the house with positive messages written to each other. You could also leave them in lunchboxes, bags or in the car.

★ Send a text to someone you haven't seen for a while and say "I love you because..."

★ Read some picture storybooks together. Take it in turns to read to each other.

★ Sit around the table as a family. Each person has a pencil and a piece of paper. Everyone has a minute or two to start writing a story. Stop. Fold your paper so the next person can only see the last line of the story. Pass the paper to the left and each person continues writing the story that they have just received. Continue until everyone has written on each piece of paper. Read the completed stories to each other.

★ During dinner, only communicate with each other using paper and pen.

★ Go to the beach and write some messages in the sand.

★ Write some fun messages to family members in your non-preferred writing hand. Leave them around the house during the week. Collect them and at the end of the week, try to figure who wrote each message.

These days, we are so connected with each other through our devices: the Internet, email, Facebook, Instagram, Twitter and even phone calls. When I completed high school, I took off in an old car with a mate on a trip around Australia. I was on a tight budget, so the only communication I had with my parents was the odd postcard home. A few years later, with an adventurous spirit and still little money, I spent nine months in Asia. Once again, only a postcard home every now and then. I spent the next few years working and traveling throughout Europe where I sent more postcards and letters home. I don't know how I would cope if my kids travelled for long periods of time with so little communication. However, those letters and postcards were really special. On returning home, my parents had kept many of them and it was a lovely way to reconnect with all the experiences that I had and all the places I was fortunate enough to visit.

> "Words are singularly the most powerful force available to humanity. We can choose to use this force constructively with words of encouragement, or destructively using words of despair. Words have energy and power with the ability to help, to heal, to hinder, to hurt, to harm, to humiliate and to humble."
>
> Yehuda Berg

What do you like to write?

Fictional fANTasy.

April Week 4

Delegation

Delegation could be thought of as giving or assigning a task to another person. It may also be giving power or responsibility to someone. Delegating a task to another person could be beneficial to both parties. Firstly, the person delegating is able to free up time. Secondly, the person taking on the task is given the responsibility of completing it, which may encourage responsibility. Delegation might be considered to be a win-win situation for us all.

Delegate the task of choosing one of the following activities to try together this week to someone else in the family.

★ Play a board game or card game and have someone delegate responsibilities, like setting up, dealing and packing up at the end. Some games, like Monopoly, require a player to be the banker. Delegate these types of tasks to others.

★ Cook a meal together and delegate different tasks. Include other jobs, like setting the table, clearing the plates at the end and washing up.

★ Go out into the garden and have a working bee. List all the tasks that need to be completed and have someone be responsible for delegating each of the tasks to others.

★ Clean the house together as a family. Somebody gets to assign each job to different family members.

★ Have someone plan a special family movie night. They will need to delegate different tasks, like setting up the movie, getting drinks, organising snacks and so forth.

★ Organise a bike ride or long walk with some friends. Delegate someone to organise the route, another organises the food and someone else the drinks. Do you need to delegate any other tasks?

★ Put on a load of washing together and delegate the different tasks from putting the washing and detergent into the machine, hanging it all out, bringing it in and then finally putting it away.

★ Consider an area inside the house that could do with a tidy up. Make a list of all the jobs that need to be completed then delegate each task to different members of the family.

★ Think about a family member or someone in the neighbourhood that could do with some help. Make a list of some things you could do to help them out and one person is to delegate each job.

★ Plan a picnic or barbeque in the park and invite some friends. Work out what food you would like to take and delegate what food you would like each other family to bring. Does someone need to bring a barbeque? What about drinks? What type of food will you need?

As I started my new role as the leader of the Year One teaching team, the beginning of the year brought on so much work, as it always does. New kids, new classes, new groups, new staff members, excursions to organise, paperwork, goal setting... the list goes on. Apart from teaching kids, there is always a lot to get through. As the leader, I had so much to do and to take it on alone would be crazy. Apart from teaching, I had a busy life at home, as everyone seems to these days. Driving Daisy to music lessons, Finn to tennis and Monty to soccer. I needed to delegate some of the task to my team. We discussed what needed to be done and then I requested that they each take on some of the jobs to help the team. This way, each person had a choice to take it on and a choice of which jobs to complete. Not only did I find that many of the jobs had been delegated, giving me more time, but also everyone experienced teamwork within the group. The tasks that needed to be completed showed up to everyone as opportunities to contribute to our team.

> "Surround yourself with the best people you can find, delegate authority, and don't interfere as long as the policy you've decided upon is being carried out." ·
>
> Ronald Reagan

I delegate you to organise the food.

Looks like I'm off to the cANTeen then.

May Week 1

Imagination

The Oxford Dictionary defines imagination as the act or power of forming a mental image of something not present to the senses or never before wholly perceived in reality. It could also be expressed as the ability to think of new and interesting ideas. Perhaps creating a picture in the mind may be another simple way of defining imagination. It seems amazing to me that young children can imagine anything, but as they grow older, they can begin to lose that ability.

But what could be the benefits of an imagination that improved with age? Some may say that it might boost intelligence and keep us younger. It may help us to transform dreams into reality, and help us to dream big. Imagination may develop and feed our creativity. Some people believe that using our imagination can help us to improve our memory and may even promote our empathy.

Here is a list of ideas to help you to boost your imagination skills. Choose one to try at home together with your family.

- ★ Invent a short story and tell everyone. You can make the whole thing up or perhaps you could embellish something that you did as a family together.

- ★ Play 'Mr. Squiggle'. One person quickly draws a squiggle on a piece of paper and passes it along for the next person to complete the drawing.

- ★ Draw some pictures in the driveway with chalk or paint brushes and water.

- ★ Get a newspaper and make the photos more interesting by adding different things to each picture.

- ★ Take a paper bag and go for a walk. Collect five or 10 different items from nature and put them into the bag. When you get home, pick out an item from your collection and tell everyone a made-up story of what the item would be if an alien found it on their planet.

- ★ Imagine you won the lottery. What would you do with the money? Discuss.

- ★ Make up some 'campfire' stories to tell each other.

- ★ Lie on the grass and look up at the clouds and tell everyone all the images you can see in the sky.

- ★ Get a box and make something with it. It could be a shoe box, a fruit box or a box from a new appliance.

- ★ Rename the members of your family and your friends. Why did you choose this new name for them?

One of the best things about teaching young children is watching them play. When they are out at recess or lunch, they'll play imaginary games, either with or without any toys. They'll be running around and acting with imaginary props and they all know exactly what is going on, which child is playing each character and what they are meant to do. I remember being a helper when my children were in kindergarten. That was a truly inspirational time in their lives where there were little boundaries, but so much to do. When they were at kinder, the teachers were not required to report on the progress of the children; they simply inspired their group of kids to explore and use their imagination to grow and develop while having loads of fun. They were wonderful times and Daisy, Finn and Monty still talk about kinder.

> "Without leaps of imagination or dreaming, we lose the excitement of possibilities. Dreaming, after all is a form of planning."
>
> Gloria Steinem

Commitment

> "You always have two choices: your commitment versus your fear."
>
> Sammy Davis, Jr

Dedication and a guarantee that you will do something you set out to achieve, no matter what, could be defined as commitment. Nothing will get in your way of achieving your goal, even when you face what seem massive challenges and encounter setbacks that may stop many others. Being committed to a goal can help to keep you focused on the outcome. It can also support us to work hard to achieve our goal and to realise success, even when we are faced with hurdles.

Jill Koenig started her first company with only $100 at the age of 25 after overcoming a life of poverty. Five years later, she was a self-made millionaire. She was quoted as saying "Commitment is the glue that bonds you to your goals."

I'll never give up looking for food.

Just look in the pANTry.

Following are some ideas to help foster commitment. Choose your favourite one to try together at home.

- ★ Set a goal for the whole family to achieve by the end of the week or month. Make a plan of how you will achieve your goal together.

- ★ Make a list of some chores that everyone in the family will do to contribute to the running of the household. Did you succeed?

- ★ Discuss all the things that you are committed to in your life. Are you committed to some more than others? Why do you think this is? Discuss.

- ★ Complete a jigsaw puzzle within a time limit that you set for yourselves.

- ★ Choose a new skill, sport or musical instrument you would like to learn. How will you achieve this?

- ★ Build a house of cards. Decide how tall you would like to make it. Was this easy or difficult for you? Was your house too low or too high?

- ★ Think about something that you would really like to save for. Make a plan and set a date as to when you will achieve your goal.

- ★ Talk about someone you know who is committed. What do you notice about them. Do you know any other people who are committed? Discuss.

- ★ Plan to do something small every day for the rest of the year. It might be something very small, but set up a checklist and mark it off every day when you do what you said you would do. Think about having someone as your coach who will help you achieve your goal.

- ★ Set a bedtime for everyone in the family for the week. Make sure everyone is in bed by the time they say they will be. Do you need to do anything to support each other?

After working in hospitality for nearly two decades, I decided to change career and to retrain as a primary school teacher. My wife, Sandi, and I moved from the east coast of Tasmania to Bendigo. I worked two jobs and started studying. Sandi was also working and studying. Not long after, Sandi fell pregnant and gave birth to Daisy as I started my second year of study. I had to be organised and I worked hard to achieve very good results. Nothing was going to get in the way of my goal of becoming a primary school teacher. And, as they say, the rest is history.

> "You need to make a commitment, and once you make it, then life will give you some answers."
>
> Les Brown

Leadership

> "The role of a creative leader is not to have all the ideas; it's to create a culture where everyone can have ideas and feel that they're valued."
>
> Ken Robinson

Many definitions of leadership can vary immensely. Some say that it is the action of leading a group or to help others achieve things they may not have thought of as possible for them. Others may define leadership as being in charge of a group of people, helping to get the best out of them. Leaders may be called 'The Boss'. But some leaders sit in the background and may appear not to be doing much.

There are so many tips and advice on how to become an influential leader. So, what really defines leadership? Is it someone who leads by example? Or is a leader someone who inspires others? Maybe, by definition, a leader is a person who is at the front. Or could a leader be someone who has a dream and gets others to believe in that dream, inspiring them to work together to achieve a common goal?

Choose one of the following ideas to try this week at home to help build leadership skills.

★ Someone is to organise a meal for the family that involves everyone doing something to help out.

★ Play 'Follow the Leader'.

★ Someone is to plan an obstacle course in the garden or at the park and organise everyone to attempt to get to the end.

★ Choose someone to be the leader. They get to select a game to play and must convince everyone else why they should all play the game with them.

★ Without talking, select a leader. The leader must silently organise everyone into groups. The others must then guess how everyone has been arranged.

★ Think about something around the house that you would like to change, clean or tidy. One person is to get everyone organised to achieve the task together.

★ Go on a bike ride or walk together that is organised by one of the younger members of the family.

★ Play 'Guess the Leader'. Someone leaves the room and a leader is chosen from the remaining group. The team follows the actions of the leader while the chosen person re-enters the room and guesses who the leader is.

★ Put names into a hat. Draw out a leader. The leader must assign everyone various jobs (including themselves) in order to clean the house.

★ A leader of the family is chosen and needs to organise a family excursion, picnic or activity to do together.

From the moment the Bridge to Bridge ride was mentioned one morning during coffee by Mikey, he was always the leader of this unforgettable event. The Bridge to Bridge (B2B) ride involved a group of guys riding from the Sydney Harbour Bridge to the Barwon Heads Bridge on bicycles covering over 1000 kilometres. Mikey was always there, seemingly in the background as others jumped on board and played their part. Never once did Mikey need to assert himself, play boss or order anyone about. He just quietly went about his business to lead the team in the planning and execution of the ride. He quietly organised the daily route and gave morning briefings before we headed off each day. Mikey lead us on the whole journey without any fuss or wanting to big note himself. He was an inspirational leader and it was a pleasure to ride with him all the way from Sydney to Barwon Heads.

> "The task of the leader is to get his people from where they are to where they have not been."
>
> Henry A. Kissinger

May Week 4

Compassion

> "If you want others to be happy, practice compassion. If you want to be happy, practice compassion."
>
> Dalai Lama

Compassionate people may see the suffering of others and want to help them in some way. The word comes from the Latin 'compassio', which means to suffer together. The Dalai Lama suggests that compassion is the key to happiness. Other benefits may include a boost to our health and longevity as well as uplifting others around us. Some believe being compassionate can even make us more attractive!

Here are a few fun ideas to try together to help foster compassion. Choose one from the list to do this week. Have fun!

- ★ Phone a relative or friend that you haven't talked to in a while.

- ★ One person acts a mood that they may not normally like such as sadness, being tired, upset or lonely. Someone else notices their mood and helps them to feel better.

- ★ Find some clothes that you don't want anymore and donate them to a charity or give them to an op shop.

- ★ Role play some of the following situations: a friend looks lonely, one of the family feels unwell, someone is tired at the end of the day, you notice a stranger fall over and hurt themselves. How do you show compassion in these situations?

- ★ Think about someone you have noticed who hasn't been as happy as they usually are. Do something kind for them to cheer them up.

- ★ Consider sponsoring a child from an underprivileged country.

- ★ Think about someone that lives near you, who might need some help. Cook them a meal or help them in the garden for an hour or so.

- ★ Next time you are at work or school, talk to someone you normally don't talk to.

- ★ Pick some flowers from your garden and give them to a stranger.

- ★ Cook a meal or a sweet treat and give it to someone else.

While teaching Year One students, we were researching toys and the impact they have on children. As a group, the kids talked about how much they loved them as any group of six and seven-year-old children would. The discussion progressed to the number of toys that each of them had. We all couldn't believe how many toys each kid had in the group. From here, an idea was born. We decided to create a project called 'The Toy Op Shop'. Tasks were listed and jobs delegated amongst the children. Posters were created and stuck up around the school. A note went into the school newsletter. Over the following few weeks, many kids from across the school brought in unwanted toys. One lunchtime, all the kids in the junior school brought in a gold coin and purchased a new toy that had been donated. They raised quite a bit of money and were so proud of their efforts. The money was donated to a local man who recently started a project that was giving portable beds to homeless people. And the left-over toys were taken to the local op shop. The students felt so proud of their efforts and their contribution to others.

> "Love and compassion are necessities, not luxuries.
> Without them humanity cannot survive."
>
> Dalai Lama

June Week 1

Time Management

> "I am definitely going to take a course on time management...
> just as soon as I can work it into my schedule."
>
> Louis E. Boone

Time management could be defined as using our time wisely, organising and dividing it between various activities. It may be the ability to use our time effectively or productively. It has been suggested that effective time management can help us to improve work-life balance and therefore increasing our happiness. Other benefits we may notice could include getting more done while reducing stress. Additionally, we may waste less time and actually create more free time, spending it where we choose to. As some people say, "Work smarter, not harder."

From the following list of ideas, choose one that may be useful to your family to help teach time management.

★ Write a list of things that you would like to achieve in an hour, either on your own or together as a family. Number them in order from first to last. Start the timer and go. Discuss what happened.

★ Write another list of things that you would love to do in an hour. Do not do any of them. After an hour, discuss how you felt.

★ Plan one night of the week when everyone goes to bed early. Did you notice anything different the next day?

★ Turn the television off for one week and see what happens.

★ Start a stopwatch and have everyone close their eyes. Open them when you think two minutes have elapsed. Write down your time. Were you close? Discuss how long two minutes felt.

★ Make a simple calendar for a week that only includes some fun things that you will do together. Make sure you include the time that you plan to do each activity.

★ Keep a record of how many hours sleep everyone gets in the week. Compare and discuss once you have collected the data.

★ Choose one day of the week when you turn off the internet, phones and television and play some games together.

★ Sit together in the house somewhere and choose a book to read. Agree on a period of time that you will read. Set a timer and read.

★ Plan a menu for the week and decide who will do what to help shop, prepare, serve each meal and also who will clean up when finished.

My wife, Sandi, is amazing at managing time. She packs so much into every day. Sandi will get up early and walk our dog, Rufus. She'll help the kids get organised and make her lunch while eating breakfast and getting ready for work. At work as a librarian, she is organised and efficient. During her lunch break, she'll manage to study or do some grocery shopping. On the way home, Sandi will make some phone calls in the car, keeping in contact with her family and friends. Then when home, Sandi will find time to go for another walk with the dog and often the kids and I will join in. Next is preparing and cooking dinner. Often, she will manage to wash some clothes and hang them out too. Some evenings during the week, Sandi will find the time to help out on the tennis club committee or to write a paper for her studies. Sandi's time management skills allow her to have more family time throughout the week.

> "My favourite things in life don't cost any money. It's really clear that the most precious resource we all have is time."
>
> Steve Jobs

June Week 2

Humility

> "The sage puts himself last and becomes first."
>
> Tao Te Ching

Humility may often be linked to modesty. Someone who is humble may understand they do not have all the answers. They may have achieved some great things; however, they rarely talk about them. When we are humble, we may have a realistic understanding of our strengths and also our weaknesses. Humility comes from the Latin word 'humilis', meaning low. It has been said that people who show humility may be able to better cope when feeling anxious. Humble leaders could be considered to be more effective as well as being liked. They may also have a lower sense of entitlement, not feeling that they are owed anything. When we show humility, we may have better relationships with others as we are more able to accept people for who they are.

Here are some ideas to help foster humility. Choose one that suits your family, try it this week and see what you discover.

- ★ Choose someone to act as the waiter for everyone during dinner. Their job is to ensure everyone has everything that they need and even more. They need to go out of their way to make sure everyone has a great time.

- ★ Perform some 'Random Acts of Kindness' to others during the week. Each night over dinner, discuss what happened and how you felt.

- ★ Do you know a famous person who has not let that fame 'go to their head'? What do you notice about them?

- ★ Talk about the people who do jobs that are often thankless and go unnoticed. Choose one of these people and thank them for doing the job that they do.

- ★ Play a card game or board game together. At the end, everyone including the winner, must be humble and thank each other for playing.

- ★ Go to the local park or beach and collect rubbish.

- ★ Talk about people you know who are humble. What is it about them that makes them humble?

- ★ What mistakes have you made recently? How did you feel when you made the mistake and how do you feel now? Do you think it is important to admit making a mistake when you do? Discuss.

- ★ Next time you are out, see how many times you can hold the door open for other people. Talk about how it made you feel. Did you notice how they felt?

- ★ Find a neighbour or friend that may be in need of some help and do some odd jobs for them, like helping in the garden, cleaning their car or taking them a meal.

Many years ago, I was fortunate enough to work in an amazing restaurant in Melbourne, called Stephanie's. The business gained many prestigious awards every year and was regarded as one of the best restaurants in Australia. While working there, the owner, Stephanie Alexander, wrote some books about food.

Eventually, she wrote 'The Cook's Companion', which became a massive seller, changing the cooking habits of many Australians. Eventually, the restaurant closed and Stephanie opened a café and cheese larder in inner city Melbourne, which became an instant success.

Not having achieved enough, Stephanie went on to change the way primary school children related to food with her Kitchen Garden Foundation. I don't see Stephanie very often, but when I do, she is always extremely humble.

> "Humility is the solid foundation of all virtues."
>
> Confucius

Courtesy

> "Courtesy costs nothing, but buys everything."
>
> Hazrat Ali Ibn Abu-Talib A.S.

Courtesy could be said to be politeness in behaviour and attitude towards others, which may include a polite remark or respectful behaviour. Courtesy requires us to think of others before thinking of ourselves, often following empathy. Teaching a child to be courteous may have them also learn respect. One of the added bonuses of showing respect and being well-mannered to others is that they are often kind in return.

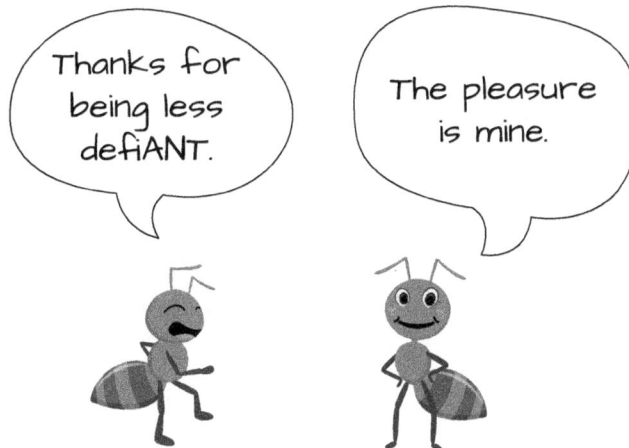

We have all experienced being treated discourteously and we may notice that our mood will often shift in an unwanted direction. On the other hand, when someone shows us courtesy, our mood may often lift and we could find ourselves being happier and showing more courtesy and respect to others. It appears to be one of those things that seems to rub off on others. As American author and philosopher Ralph Waldo Emerson said; "As we are, so we do; and as we do, so is it done to us; we are the builders of our fortunes."

Try one of the following ideas together with your family to help build courtesy and remember to have fun!

- ★ Play a game where someone asks another person for them to do something without saying please or making eye-contact. They must ignore them until they ask while making eye-contact and also saying please. Remember to thank the person for completing the task.

- ★ Play a variation on 'Simon Says' where everyone only does what Simon says if Simon says "please".

- ★ Cut out a heart shape on some paper and fold it into four parts. On each part write four different ways you can show courtesy to others.

- ★ Have a competition to see how many times each person can open a door for someone else in a day or over the week.

- ★ Google 'funny apology notes from kids' and read them together.

- ★ Have one person act as the waiter during dinner, serving dinner and clearing the table at the end.

- ★ Write a thank-you note to someone who has done something for you recently.

- ★ Play some board games and card games together.

- ★ 'Do to others as you would have others do to you.' Talk about what this means to you. Does this include courtesy and manners?

- ★ While eating dinner, discuss table manners and etiquette. What is important to you? What is not so important?

I have been riding a bike since I was a child. I always rode to school and I've always ridden to work whenever I have been able to. Bike riding has always been a part of my transportation and exercise. Over recent years in Australia, there has been much publicity about cyclists taking over the roads and motorists not sharing the roads. The media often report about the divide between the two parties. Apparently, motorists hate cyclists and cyclists are being bullied by motorists. In all the years that I've been riding, I have found that there is such a very small number of motorists that have been rude or aggressive to me on my bike. The majority of car and truck drivers are amazingly courteous. They will often wait behind me to pass, overtake giving a large amount of room and give a polite wave on the way past.

> "All doors open to courtesy."
>
> Thomas Fuller

June Week 4

Feedback

Feedback could be designed to help us improve our performance or refine a project we are working on. It should be designed to motivate us to progress. There is a skill in both giving and receiving feedback. It may require us to be empathetic when giving feedback as we need to consider how the person receiving the feedback may react and how they may feel. When receiving feedback, we might need to listen to the message about the feedback and not take it personally, but rather think about our performance or behaviour. I have often found feedback helpful; however, I always consider who is giving the feedback and why it is being given to me.

Here is a list of ideas designed to help give and receive feedback. Choose one that is the best fit for your family and have fun with it this week.

★ Give feedback about dinner using 'Three Stars and a Wish'. Say three things you liked and one thing you would like to change.

★ Everyone has a piece of paper and some coloured pencils. Draw a terrible picture of something you like to do or a place you like to go. Show your picture to everyone and then listen to their feedback.

★ Play a board game or card game together. At the end, give feedback to others about how well they played.

★ Everyone is to create something using the same limited amount of materials in a small amount of time. At the end, tell everyone what you like about what they made.

★ Create a 'Feedback Tree' where everyone can add their feedback about your family and your home.

★ Dress up and stand in front of the family. Everyone is to give you feedback about some things they like about what you are wearing and also tell you something that they think you should change.

★ Play 'Mr. Squiggle' and offer feedback to everyone when they have completed their drawing.

★ Google 'Austin's Butterfly' and watch the short video together.

★ When you see someone do something you like, simply say "I like how you..."

★ Draw a picture of something you like. Everyone is to give some feedback about your picture and then you are to draw it again. Listen to feedback again and draw the picture for the third time. Compare your three pictures.

When I'm teaching a class of children, if I ever want honest feedback about how the lesson is going, all I have to do is ask the kids. I'll sometimes check in with them by asking what they liked about a lesson and what they didn't like. I may also ask what was useful about the lesson. Kids will always give it to me straight. Sometimes, I don't even need to ask. If I look at the group, I can tell when I've been talking too much as their eyes start glazing over or they become restless. At the same time, it's very easy to see if the children are engaged. They are focused and on task when working on their own, or when doing partner or group work, there is a 'working noise' in the classroom as the kids are collaborating.

> "Feedback is the breakfast of champions."
>
> Ken Blanchard

July Week 1

Problem Solving

> "Problem solving is hunting. It is savage pleasure and we are born to it."
>
> Thomas Harris

What shows up as a problem for one person may show up as an opportunity for another. A problem could be regarded as something that is unwelcome or unwanted and needs to be dealt with or overcome. Mathematical problems or conundrums may appear as a challenge to be solved. Problem solving may involve working through a series of steps to find a solution. And, once you have solved a problem, you may look backwards and wonder why you thought the problem was actually a problem. Can you imagine what it would be like if problems always showed up as opportunities?

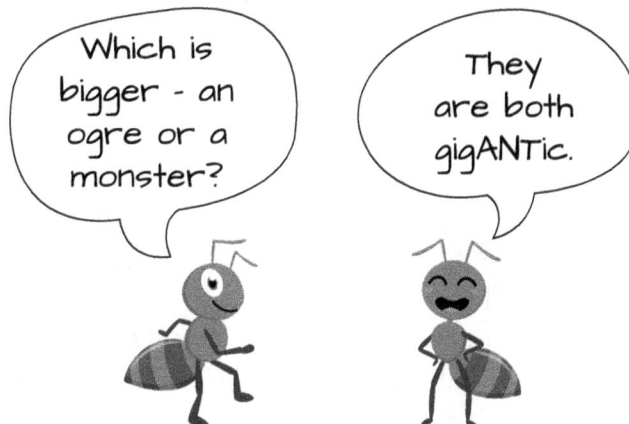

Which is bigger - an ogre or a monster?

They are both gigANTic.

Here are some fun activities to try together as a family this week. Choose the one that best suits you all.

★ Work out what to have for dinner tonight without going shopping. Only use what you already have at home.

★ Find a new direction to travel to work/school/the shops. What did you discover? What would you see differently if you took this route?

★ Play 'Celebrity Heads' or 'Guess Who' together.

★ As a family, Google 'problem solving for children' and work together to find solutions to the challenges you discover.

★ Imagine being stranded on a deserted island. What would be the five things you would take with you? Remember, there is no electricity on the island. Talk about some of the things you would do to survive.

★ Talk about something that you usually do in your family. Then consider a change and say, "What if…" and complete the sentence. Discuss.

★ Get out a deck of cards and play a game you know together. Then, with your playing cards, learn a new game and play it as a family.

★ Stand next to each other with your hands beside you. At the same time, everyone reaches in to the middle and holds hands. Together, you need to untangle the knot of hands without breaking the chain. The idea is to finish in a linked circle.

★ Build a tower using only spaghetti and marshmallows or newspaper and sticky tape. How tall can you make it? Can you make a bridge with the same materials? How far can your bridge span?

★ Set a problem for someone else in the family to solve. Can anyone else solve it?

Many kids I teach in primary school come up to me with their problems or issues. I always listen to their concerns and comfort them if needed. The next thing that I'll usually do is ask them, "How are you going to solve your problem?" I listen to them as they form their ideas and more often than not, they know what to do. Sometimes, I'll give them a little guidance if needed, but this doesn't happen very often. I always assume that each child has the ability to deal with any issue they have, and most often, they do.

> "The best way to escape from a problem is to solve it."
>
> Brendan Francis

Being Energetic

> "An energetic man will succeed where an indolent
> one would vegetate and inevitably perish."
>
> Jules Verne

Loads of energy and vitality – who wouldn't want more of this? Some people seem to have lots more energy than others. But, is this energy limited? Or, are we able to create energy from nothing, even when we are tired? Have you ever noticed that when you are feeling flat and worn out and don't seem to have the energy to do anything, something happens? Maybe a friend turns up and gives you an offer you can't refuse and somehow, you are re-energised. You all of a sudden, become full of vitality.

I am full of energy.

You are looking rather vibrANT.

Can you imagine what it would be like if we could be enthusiastic and full of energy whenever we chose? If we were able to create energy out of nothing, what things could we achieve?

Some of the benefits of us being energetic could be simply getting more stuff done. Others may want to be around us more as this energy can be contagious. As German music group, Snap, sang in 1990, "I Got the Power!"

Try one of the following to help create some more energy within your family. Get to it and have some fun!

- ★ Get up early and see the sunrise.
- ★ Hold a 'trick show' where everyone gets to show any tricks or stunts that they can do.
- ★ Blow up a balloon and play balloon tennis, soccer or any other sport you fancy.
- ★ Hold a family Olympics event in the back yard.
- ★ Go to a lake, river or to the beach and skip stones in the water.
- ★ Make an obstacle course in the garden or at the local park.
- ★ Put your feet into two empty tissue boxes and go indoor skating.
- ★ Have a pillow fight.
- ★ Make a paper plane and fly it at the local park.
- ★ Go for a bike ride or long walk together.

Being a primary school teacher takes energy, particularly if you are teaching younger primary school children. Some days at work, I am tired and may not be in the mood. In the past, I have found that if I carry this mood into the classroom, the children will almost mimic my mood and the day drags on. I have discovered that if I create an energetic mood, usually by becoming more physically active, the children will become more energetic. They will then work with more enthusiasm and produce better results while actually having fun. And, I have heaps more fun too!

"In this very real world, good doesn't drive out evil. Evil doesn't drive out good. But the energetic displaces the passive."

William Bernbach

July Week 3

Sense of Humour

> "Humour is by far the most significant activity of the human brain."
>
> Edward de Bono.

This is a very important and serious life skill. And I mean really serious. What would life be like if we couldn't have a laugh? A little giggle or one of those laughs we have with a friend that you can't stop laughing with each other and your stomach is in pain. "Please stop. No more." But the laughing continues.

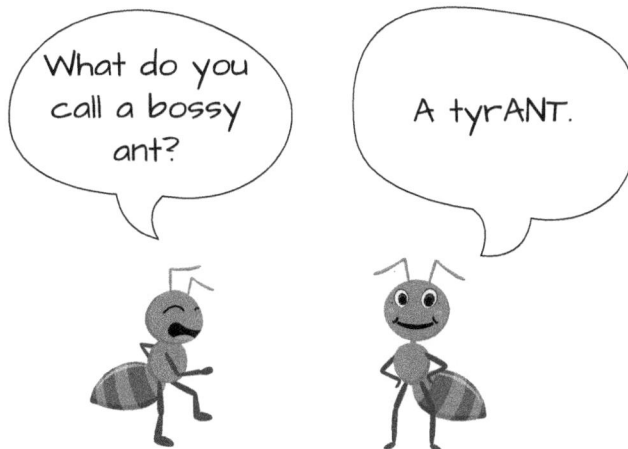

People who have a great sense of humour may often be surrounded by others. They can be magnetic. There have been loads of studies into the benefits of laughter and how it does stuff to your brain. But, who needs studies? We all know what it's like to laugh and have fun. Laughing can be a great way for us to cope with stress and from which we can also gain many health benefits. Apparently, some scientists believe that it can lower blood pressure and aid muscle relaxation. Mahatma Ghandi was quoted as saying 'If I had no sense of humour, I would long ago have committed suicide.' But all of this sense of humour business sounds way to serious to me!

Have a look at the following list of things to do to help boost your sense of humour at home. Choose your favourite and have a good laugh along the way.

★ Think about something funny that happened to you a when you were younger. Tell your family about it and why it still makes you laugh.

★ Go to the library and get some joke books and tell jokes to each other.

★ Have a staring competition – the person who keeps a straight face the longest wins.

★ Watch a funny movie together.

★ Talk about funny people you know. What makes them funny? Why do you laugh at them? Talk about some things that they did to make you laugh.

★ Look through a family photo album and find photos that make you laugh.

★ Make up some really bad 'Dad Jokes'. Any joke that gets a laugh gets one point.

★ Play 'Mirror Dance' where one person moves and the other mimics their partner as if they were their reflection.

★ Get a newspaper and draw on the pictures of people to make them look funny.

★ Put on some music and do some silly dancing together.

One of my best school friends, Zdrav, is a very funny person. We are always laughing and being silly when we are together, despite our age. We have always laughed together and we always will. We live a long distance apart, however when we catch up, the laughs and silliness start immediately. Our kids and wives just roll their eyes as we break into our immature behaviour. Every time we are on the phone together, my wife, Sandi, and our kids know who I am talking to, as does his family. Once we get going, there is no stopping us. I start laughing at his laugh, and he at mine. Sometimes, we just need to hang up the phone to recover from the pain in our stomachs. I find having a good laugh like this is often very therapeutic.

> "The problem with having a sense of humour is often that people you use it on aren't in a very good mood."
>
> Lou Holtz

Honesty

> "The secret of life is honesty and fair dealing. If you can fake that, you've got it made."
>
> Groucho Marx

Honesty and truth seem to be very connected. They both could be regarded as being free from deceit and being sincere. It may also mean not hiding the truth and being genuine. Some believe that we must be honest to ourselves before we are honest to others. Some of the benefits of us being honest may include authenticity and courage. Honest people could be seen to be more caring and may also attract other honest people into their lives. Honesty could help us to promote more trusting relationships and peace of mind, and may also benefit our personal health. As Benjamin Franklin said, honesty is the best policy.

Choose one of the following ideas to try this week to help foster honesty in your family.

★ Discuss what honesty means to you. How does your view differ from others in the family? Talk about how you are honest. Have you ever been dishonest? How did you feel?

★ Play 'Two Truths and a Lie'. Each person takes a turn at saying three things about themselves; two are true and one is a lie. Everyone else must guess which the lie is.

★ Everyone is to hold something in their hand that cannot be seen. In turn, each person says what is in their hand. Everyone else must guess if they are telling the truth or telling a lie.

★ Should you always tell the truth? Is there a time when you should not tell someone the truth? Discuss.

★ What would you do if you found $10? What about $100? Or even $1000? Is there an amount that you should keep and an amount that you shouldn't keep?

★ Who is someone you know who is always honest? How do you know that they never lie?

★ Next time you are driving in the car together, tell everyone some things that you 'saw' on the trip. Everyone else needs to guess if you are being honest or not.

★ How do you know if someone is not telling you the truth? What do you notice about your face or your body when you are not telling the truth to someone?

★ Place a variety of coins into a bag that you can't see into. Everyone must take some coins from the bag without showing anybody else. Each person must say how many coins they have and everyone else must guess if they are being honest or not.

★ Play a board or card game and try to cheat without being caught. What did you notice?

I remember riding my bike around with some friends when I was about 10. We stopped outside an army disposals shop and went in for a look at all the outdoor equipment they had. For some unknown reason, which to this day I cannot explain, I picked up a small fishing tackle box, put it under my arm and ran out of the shop without paying. And I didn't even like fishing! As I tried to jump on my bike, the shop owner caught me and took me back inside. Panicked and worried, I just started to cry. I felt terrible. Not only for the trouble that may follow, but for taking something that did not belong to me. I remember apologising many times before the owner called my dad. When he arrived, I think the shopkeeper saw that he didn't need to punish me – I was taking care of the punishment on my own.

> "Achievements on the golf course are not what matters, decency and honesty are what matter."
>
> Tiger Woods

Dreaming

> "Man is a genius when he is dreaming."
>
> Akira Kurosawa

What is the difference between imagination and dreaming? Do we dream in our sleep and imagine when we are awake? Or could a dream be a goal that may seem incredibly difficult to achieve? Maybe one that could be reached against all odds? A goal where others wish you luck that somehow doesn't feel genuine? I wonder if all those people who have achieved great things in their lives were dreamers? As they say, if you are going to dream, dream big.

I wonder what the benefits of dreaming could be? Perhaps when we dream, we can see that anything may be possible; dreaming may allow us to remove any perceived barriers in front of our goal. It may allow us to see the end result and then we create the pathway there and bring our dream to life.

You look very dreamy.

Do you mean I look vacANT?

From the following suggestions, choose the best one for your family to do together to help become wonderful dreamers.

- ★ If you could have anything, what would it be? Talk together about what could be possible. Do you think that anything is impossible?

- ★ Who do you know that has followed their dreams? What do you think they did to bring their dreams to reality?

- ★ Lots of people say to 'follow your dreams'. But what happens if you start to follow them and you get stuck? How could you keep going despite hitting hurdles along the way? Discuss.

- ★ Have you ever been caught day-dreaming at school or work? Talk about what happened and how you felt.

- ★ What would you do if you won the lottery? Dream up some crazy ideas of how to spend your winnings.

- ★ Draw a picture of what you would look like when you achieve one of your dreams. Who would be near you? What would your face look like? What else would be in the picture? When finished, hang your picture where you can see it.

- ★ Where do you dream about travelling to? Look on the internet and dream up an incredible family holiday.

- ★ Have you ever had a dream that has come true? Have any of your dreams nearly come true? Talk together during dinner time.

- ★ What could your world look like in the future, if all of your dreams came true?

- ★ Find a quiet place where you can see a long way and stare off into the distance. Pick something and focus on it and let you mind wander. Talk about what you noticed. How did your body feel during the experience? How does your body feel now?

As a child, a friend always dreamed of becoming a professional drummer. He wanted to be the best that he could and often people would tell him that he probably wouldn't succeed. Many others told him that his dreams were very big and not many people managed to play drums in a successful band. Andy stuck to his goal, working hard and following his passion. He didn't listen to others who told him it would be difficult. And now, he is regarded as one of Australia's best drummers and plays in an amazingly successful rock band.

> "Dreams, if they're any good, are always a little bit crazy."
>
> Ray Charles

August Week 2

Listening

> "Most of the successful people I've known are the ones who do more listening than talking."
>
> Bernard Baruch

People often confuse hearing and listening. When I was a kid, Mum would often ask if I was listening to her and I would reply with a 'yes'. However, looking back I'm sure that, sometimes I was actually listening to her and other times I just heard her. When researching different definitions of the word 'listening', the common themes seem to be paying attention or taking notice of something being said. The word 'listen' comes from the Old English 'hlysnan' which means 'to pay attention to'. Whereas hearing could be defined as noticing a sound, but not necessarily paying attention to it. So, is it that we hear noise; however, we listen to music?

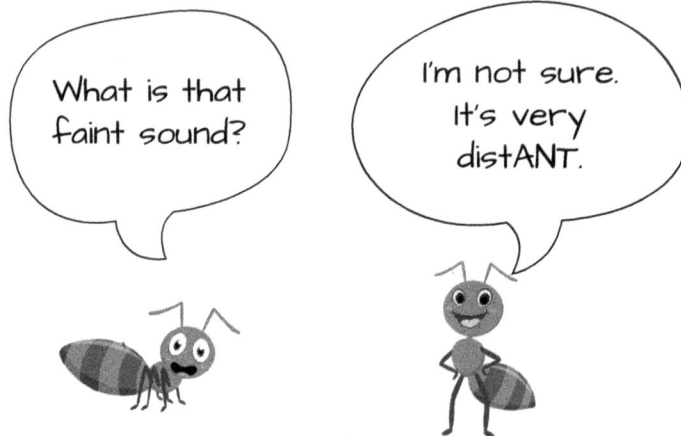

What is that faint sound?

I'm not sure. It's very distANT.

Some of the benefits of developing our listening skills could include an improvement with problem solving, productivity and being able to create healthier interpersonal relationships. If we have well-developed listening skills, we may also find that we are able to save time and perhaps be more patient and respected. As Bryant H. McGill was quoted as saying, 'One of the most sincere forms of respect is actually listening to what another has to say.'

Choose your favourite from the following suggestions to try this week to help become better listeners.

★ Make a telephone with some string and two tin cans. Use them to talk to a partner.

★ Give each other simple verbal instructions to follow. As everyone gets better, increase the number of instructions.

★ Go for a walk to the park or beach and sit quietly and listen to all the sounds. Write down what you hear then share your discoveries.

★ Play 'musical chairs' together. As the game progresses, turn the volume down lower and lower.

★ One person gets an item and describes it to others. Everyone needs to draw what is being described.

★ Play 'Chinese Whispers' together.

★ Make a list of some possible sounds that you may hear in your local environment. Go on a sound hunt and see how many of the sounds you can actually hear.

★ Is there a difference between listening and hearing? Discuss.

★ Watch a movie together with the volume turned down as low as you can all manage.

★ Hide a phone somewhere in the house and then ring the number. Who can find the phone first? Try again, but this time turn the volume down lower. How low can you turn the volume down?

My dad is the most amazing listener I've ever met. Whenever we spend time together, he doesn't just listen to what I'm saying, he listens to my mood, he listens to the possibilities that are available for me, he listens to who I really am as a person. Sometimes, I think that he knows me better than I actually know myself. He has spent most of his working life working as a counsellor, coach and hypnotherapist. He listens to his clients' concerns and guides them to find solutions to them. Listening is a large part of his work and he has taught me a lot about listening to others. It is always such a pleasure to spend time with him, talking and listening to each other.

> "Listening is such a simple act. It requires us to be present, and that takes practice, but we don't have to do anything else. We don't have to advise, or coach, or sound wise. We just have to be willing to sit there and listen."
>
> Margaret J. Wheatley

Motivation

> **"**
> "It always seems impossible until it's done."
> Nelson Mandel
> **"**

At times, some tasks seem so difficult to start. I can always find better things to do or very good reasons to procrastinate. When I am in this mood, I'll often feel heavy and tired, which adds to make the task even more challenging. Some days, I just stop and decide not to start. When I consciously do make the decision to begin, I will just start. Often, I don't really know what to do, so I'll just do something. That something gives me the start. If I have an end goal and have made a start, then I'm away. The next thing to help me achieve my end goal is to break the larger tasks into smaller, achievable parts. I will work out how much I will do each day and calculate a date that I will have my project complete. And to help me, I'll sometimes enroll a friend to help me stick to my commitment. I'll let them know how much I will get done each week and then keep them informed. All this helps me to get a large project complete.

When we are motivated, we may be able to complete projects or tasks without supervision or encouragement. We stick to our word and complete something by a date, even when things become challenging. If we are motivated, we may be able to get more done in less time. We may also find that we are way more efficient with our time. When we can see a goal in sight and we are motivated to achieve that goal, it seems that nothing can stop us getting there.

From the suggestions below, choose one that best suits your family to do this week to help you become more motivated.

★ Set yourself a goal that you can achieve by the end of the week. How will you achieve your goal? Do you need to break it down into smaller steps? At the end of the week when you have achieved your goal, discuss what you did to help you. Support each other so you all achieve your goals.

★ Choose a day where everyone wakes up early and goes for a walk together before breakfast. During breakfast, discuss how you felt and what motivated you to get up early.

★ What food do you really love that you find really hard to resist if it is placed in front of you? Talk about how you might stop eating that food for a week. Do you think you could stop eating it for a month? Consider setting a food challenge for yourself.

★ Discuss what motivates you to achieve a goal. What do you do when the going gets tough? What can you do if you feel like giving up?

★ Talk about someone you know who is successful. How do you think they remained motivated to achieve their goals? Do you think they had tough times and they almost gave up?

★ Play some card and/or board games together. At the end, discuss the importance of winning the games you just played. How important was it to win the games? Did you really want to win? Or did you not really care? Why do so many people want to win? Discuss why you think that so many people are motivated to win.

★ Talk about some of your bad habits. Do you think that you could stop doing one of your bad habits? What do you need to put in place to ensure that you stick to your plan?

★ Plan a long walk or bike ride that you would like to do together and set a date. Complete your challenge no matter what gets in the way.

★ If you could have anything in your life, what would that be? Do you think this dream is possible? If so, how could you achieve it? Or, is this dream impossible? Discuss.

★ Plan seven different things you will do together as a family for the week. Record them and make sure that you do everything you say you will do together.

Every weekday morning for the past 10 years, I have set my alarm for 5:30am and woken, dressed and ridden my bike with friends. I ride for an hour and cover about 30km, often along the spectacular coast of Thirteenth Beach. Summer mornings are often warm and sunrises can be spectacular. As the temperature starts to cool in Autumn, the number of riders in our group can decrease. Winter can be cold and wet, but invigorating at the same time. And spring will bring the winds and warmer air. Exercise, friendship and often coffee are all part of the morning ride. The only thing that will stop me from an early morning weekday ride is pouring rain.

> "Once something is a passion, the motivation is there."
>
> Michael Schumacher

Non-Verbal Communication

> "
> "People may hear your words, but they feel your attitude."
> John C. Maxwell
> "

Non-verbal communication could be defined as communicating without spoken language and may include gestures, body positions and facial expressions, which together is often called body language. Non-verbal communication may take into account different cultural backgrounds. It could also include personal space, voice, eye contact, gestures, touch and a range of other things.

Communication researchers have suggested that many more moods and intentions are transferred non-verbally than verbally. Often, non-verbal messages can complement spoken language and it can be a wonderful substitute for words, particularly if there is noise or distance to hinder communication. As the well-known proverb states: actions speak louder than words.

Being able to read non-verbal communication could help us to be more mindful of others, adjusting our conversations as we go with more ease, perhaps even creating a verbal dance with another. It may also help us to build more harmonious and honest relationships with others.

Here is a list of some things to try together to help foster non-verbal communication skills. Choose your favourite and give it a go.

★ During dinner, have a conversation around the table without using any words.

★ Take turns to use your body to show different emotions, such as happiness, frustration, compassion, anger, unhappy, disappointed, embarrassment, etc. Have others guess what emotion you are creating.

★ Play 'Simon Says' and the person giving the instructions says what to do and does it with the group. However, sometimes the person gives the instruction but does it differently to what is said. For example, "Simon Says, put your hands on your head," while they put their hands on their shoulders. See what happens. Does it get easier as time goes on?

★ One person tells a story of something that happened to them during the day. The first time, their partner needs to be a 'good listener'. Next, they tell another story and the partner needs to be a 'poor listener'. What did you notice each time? How did you feel? What does a 'good listener' look like and what does a 'poor listener' look like?

★ Everyone writes down a command on a piece of paper so that nobody else can see it. Pass the command to the left. The person who has received the command must get the next person on their left to do what it says on the paper without talking.

★ Play 'Charades' together.

★ Use your hands and/or body to show different words, such as good, okay, no good, yes, stop, wait, etc. Have others guess what you are saying. What other words can you say without speaking?

★ Take it in turns to say how you are feeling, but have your body language be different to what you say. For example, "I'm really happy," but your face is showing anger. What do you notice?

★ Play a board game or card game together without talking.

★ Google 'Non-Verbal Communication' images. Talk about what you think each picture means. Have a go at mimicking some of the images.

Many years ago, I left Australia to travel the world. The first stop was South East Asia where I ended up spending over six months. I loved experiencing the different people and cultures. The food was amazing and it felt like every day was a new adventure. Traveling on buses, trains, trucks and in cars with the locals was such an experience. I managed to get to some very remote and unexplored places in the late-'80s. Many people did not speak any English and I certainly spoke very little of their language. I remember being in a small village in Thailand and I became aware that I desperately needed to go to the toilet. I could not find any signs that would point me in the direction I was looking for and there were no trees to stand behind to relieve myself. In desperation, I put my hand between my legs and made a long 'sssssss' noise to a small group of locals. They all started to laugh loudly, but knew what I needed, so someone pointed. I ran and made it just in time.

> "What you do speaks so loud that I cannot hear what you say."
>
> Ralph Waldo Emerson.

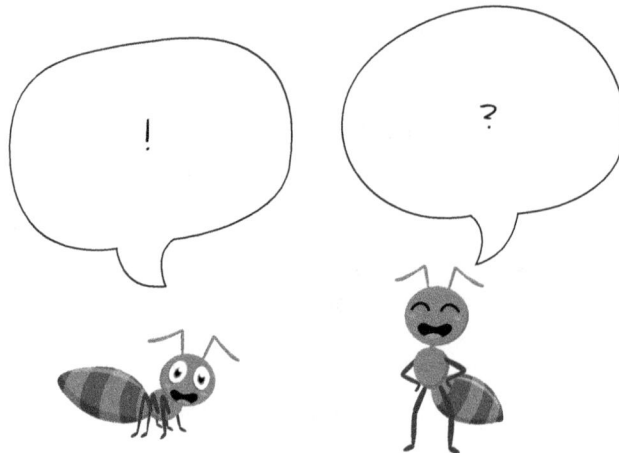

Organisation

> "Science is organized knowledge. Wisdom is organized life."
>
> Immanuel Kant

You might think that an organised person has a tidy house and a neat desk. Their bag may have different and ordered compartments or they may have a daily schedule that they stick to. You might see an organised person using lists. You wouldn't expect an organised person to be chaotic or messy, but they may be structured and logical.

One of the benefits of us being organised could be the reduction of our stress levels, which could lead to health issues. Other positive benefits for us could include being able to create more time to do things we really want to do. It may help us financially and also assist us in achieving our goals. As Benjamin Franklin

is reported to have said, "If you want something done, ask a busy person." But, is a busy person organised?

This week, choose one of the following to help foster the skill of organisation. Have fun getting organised!

★ Find a drawer or cupboard in the house and tidy it up. Take all the unwanted stuff to the op shop and neatly arrange the items you want to keep.

★ As a family, plan a meal together. Who will cook? Who will help? Who will do the shopping? Who will serve? Who will clear the table? Who will wash up? After the meal, discuss what you noticed.

★ Find some unwanted toys that you don't use anymore and give them to some family friends with younger children.

★ Discuss areas where each of you think that you are disorganised. Choose one area in which you would like to become more organised. Then write a list of the things that you will do to make the changes that you want.

★ Write a list of the things that you would like to achieve today/tomorrow/ this week. Tick each item off as you do them. What did you notice about having a list? How did it feel to tick off each item?

★ Play card games that require you to have your cards sorted or categorised in certain ways.

★ Blindfold someone and give them some random items to sort into different categories. Once complete, have them take off the blindfold and talk about why they grouped items together.

★ Get a pad of sticky notes and use them as reminders for the week. Stick them in places where you think you will notice them. At the end of the week, talk about what you discovered.

★ Tidy your clothes cupboards and drawers. Take any items of clothing that you don't need or haven't worn for a while to the op shop.

★ Plan a family picnic and take some games to play while you are there.

I have always been an organised person. I use a diary and when the electronic version came in, I was in heaven. I remember someone seeing my diary once and commenting how busy I must have been. It may have seemed that way, but it's how I remember things and how I manage to keep my word and to do what I say I'll do. If I can't complete a task by a certain time, I'll move it to the next day. At the end of each day, my diary is clear and my day is complete. Sometimes, things may move a few times before they are actually completed; however, they usually get done.

Being organised can help us stay on top of things and to keep our promises. It will help us to keep our integrity and most definitely will help us save a load of time.

> "Electricity is really just organized lightning."
>
> George Carlin

Saying "No"

> "The art of leadership is saying no, not saying yes. It is very easy to say yes."
>
> Tony Blair

Sometimes, saying 'No' can be difficult. Often, we may feel like we need to give a reason to justify why we are giving a 'No' as an answer. Some people may find that a 'No' could disappoint or hurt someone, it may be seen as rejection or it could even cause conflict. Whereas a 'Yes' can often be an easier response to give. But, is it possible to give a 'No' and have the relationship continue as it has always been? I find it interesting that we can often feel that a 'No' with an excuse is similar to a 'Yes'.

One of the benefits for us of being able to say 'No' to someone without giving a story or an excuse may be that we are able to be more honest. It may save

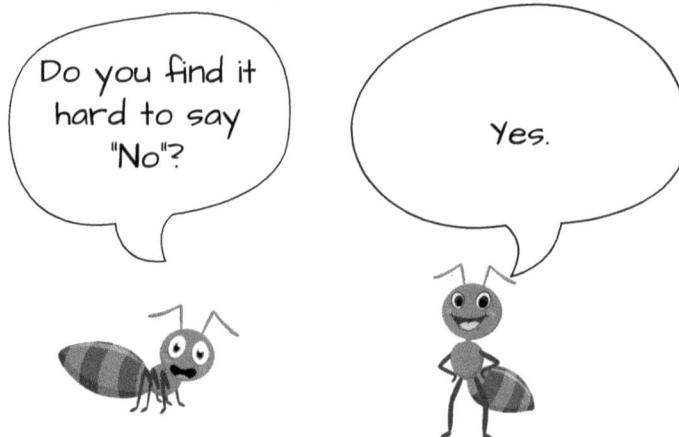

future grief or issues and it may also save us time and help us to maintain our integrity.

Following are some ideas to help you to learn to say 'No' more often. Choose your favourite to try at home this week. Or, if you prefer, say 'No' and don't do any of them!

★ Write a list of questions for which you are sure the answer will be 'Yes'. Ask them to a partner and they must respond with a 'No'.

★ Get something from around the house and 'sell' it to everyone in the family. Your job is to tell them all why this item is so wonderful, what they would benefit from having it and let them know it's even free! You then ask someone if they would like it and they need to respond with, "Thank you for the offer, but no."

★ Make a simple request of someone. The person receiving the request needs to make reasons why they will not follow your request. Continue to give reasons until you can't think of any more. Now, make the same simple request, but this time, the person receiving the request can only say "No" without giving a reason. Talk about how your experience differed between giving a reason and just saying "No".

★ When do you find it hard to say "No" to somebody? Have you ever said "Yes" because saying "No" was too hard for you? Discuss.

★ Get out some tasty treats that you all like to eat. Have someone offer them around and you must answer with a "No". What happened? Did anyone give in and say "Yes"?

★ Take it in turns to say "No" in as many different ways as you can. How many different ways can you say "No" without using your voice?

★ What is 'peer group pressure'? Have you ever been in a situation where a group of people have tried to get you to do something that made you feel uncomfortable or you thought it was wrong? Discuss.

★ Ask someone a question that you would normally expect them to say "Yes" to. The job of the person listening to the question is to first say "No, thanks," but remain facing the person. The person must ask the same question again a few more times and the respondent says, "No, thanks" each time. This time, ask the same question, but the person responding says, "No, thanks," then smiles and turns and walks away. What did you both notice that was different this time?

★ Have someone ask you to do something, and you must give a "No". They must ask why and you will need to respond with, "Because I said no." What did you notice?

★ Play a game where someone offers everyone something that they would all really like. Everyone needs to continue to say "No". If someone says "Yes", then they are out of the game. Continue until the last person in the game who has not said "Yes" is crowned the winner. Now, you can ask them if they still want what was on offer. See how they respond.

Kids will always ask their parents for things. Things to do, things to have, things to eat, things to borrow. My three kids are no different. Sometimes, the kids will get a straight-out "Yes" from me, sometimes they'll get a "Yes, if you do this first," they may get a "No, because....." or even a straight-out "No" without any reason. This is how it also works for me in the classroom when I'm teaching children. One thing I've come to understand is sometimes, it isn't what my actual response is. The kids actually get when I really mean "No" and when there is room for negotiation. I think it comes from the mood that I'm generating and if I really mean it. When I really mean "No", there is rarely any attempt to negotiate. However, sometimes negotiation is a good thing.

> ""No" is a complete sentence and so often we forget that. When we don't want to do something, we can simply smile and say no. We don't have to explain ourselves, we can just say "No". Early on my journey, I found developing the ability to say no expanded my ability to say yes and really mean it. My early attempts at saying no were often far from graceful, but with practice even my no came from a place of love. Love yourself enough to be able to say yes or no."
>
> Susan Gregg

Friendliness

> " "A friend is someone who gives you total freedom to be yourself."
>
> Jim Morrison

Being friendly could be defined as being kind or pleasant and not hostile. Synonyms include affectionate, chummy, helpful, loving and welcoming. Friendliness can help us to make a difference in the lives of others. It can make others and ourselves feel good and being friendly to others will often have them return the friendliness. Often, friendly people will not be alone and their lives may be less stressful. Some people believe that this type of person will sleep better than others and will also be healthier, getting sick less often. Whatever other people believe, being friendly just feels really good and also makes a difference to others. How can we all go wrong!

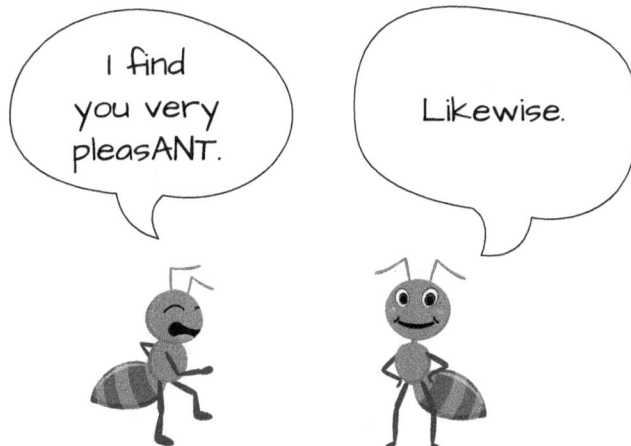

Here are some ideas to choose from this week. Pick your favourite and give it a go. Have some friendly fun together.

★ Walk down to the local shops and have a conversation with somebody in one of the stores. When you get home, talk about what happened and how you felt.

★ Discuss what you think a friendly person does. How do they act and what does their face look like? Who do you know that is often friendly?

★ Give some compliments to friends or members of the family. How did it make you feel? Did you notice a change in the person you gave a compliment to?

★ Go for a walk at the local park or beach. Every time you pass someone, smile and say "Hello".

★ Next time you are communicating with someone, talk about lots of great and happy things. Then, start to complain about other things. Did you discover anything?

★ Have one person use an electronic device, like a phone or tablet while you are trying to be friendly towards them. Repeat the same activity but this time without the electronic device. Did you notice anything different?

★ Complete a 'random act of kindness' to a stranger and then talk to them. What did you notice?

★ Do you think it is important to be friendly? What do you think would be some benefits of being friendly?

★ Start a conversation with someone and find out about them. What do they like to do? What are they passionate about? What are their dreams for their future?

★ Who is the friendliest person you know? Why do you think they are so friendly? What kinds of things do they do that are friendly?

Recently, a friend invited Sandi and I to dine in his well-regarded and highly-awarded restaurant in Melbourne. We were very excited and looked forward to the evening for quite a few months. From the moment we arrived, we were treated as if we were friends. It was evident that every staff member was so happy to be working in this restaurant on a Saturday night. The warmth and friendliness shown to us was truly amazing and we had never met any one of his team before. It was also obvious that the staff treated everyone dining there with the same kindness and warmth. The attitude and caring nature of everyone added to the truly creative and amazing food we had that unforgettable night.

> "A good motto is: use friendliness but do not use your friends."
>
> Frank Crane

Self-Efficacy

> "
>
> "The man who says he can, and the man who says he cannot... are both correct."
>
> Confucius
>
> "

According to Wikipedia, 'psychologist Albert Bandura has defined self-efficacy as one's belief in one's ability to succeed in specific situations or accomplish a task. Our sense of self-efficacy can play a major role in how we approach goals, tasks, and challenges.' It could also be said that when we believe that we can do something, we are more likely to be able to actually do it. It could be said that self-confidence is both self-esteem and self-efficacy combined. Some believe that self-efficacy helps us to remain calm when approaching challenging or difficult tasks and may also help us to improve well-being within ourselves.

Can you win the competition?

As long as I'm an entrANT, anything is possible.

High self-efficacy may also enable us to set higher personal goals and we may be more likely to experiment with ideas. However, having too high a level of self-efficacy could be a cause of over-confidence and becoming blind to any personal weaknesses. As Albert Bandura said, 'to succeed, one cannot afford to be a realist.'

Try one of the following to help promote self-efficacy this week with your family.

★ Help to cook a challenging meal one night. First, have someone tell you that it is too difficult for you to do. Think about how you felt. Then, have the same person encourage you and tell you that you can do it. Did you feel any different?

★ Think about something that you find challenging. Sit down and slump into your chair. Say all the reasons why you cannot complete this task. Next, stand up straight and push out your chest. Say all the reasons why you can complete this task. What did you notice?

★ Talk about times when you have found something challenging and you became stuck. If you were in the same situation again, how could you change your situation so you become unstuck and complete the challenging task?

★ Write a list of all the things that you are good at. Talk about why you are good at these things and why you like to do them.

★ Set some achievable, short-term goals. Once you have achieved them, talk about how you felt.

★ Do you think you are good at maths or not very good? Have you heard anyone say that they are not good at maths? Discuss.

★ Interview a family member and have them list all of your strengths. What did you notice and how did you feel?

★ Have you ever noticed yourself remaining calm when faced with a challenge where others around you may become stressed or nervous? What about the other way around? Discuss.

★ Are there any goals that you are sure you will achieve no matter what? What is it about yourself and these goals that make you so sure you will not fail?

★ Help someone around the house with something that you have never done before. Have the person praise your effort, not your ability. Were you able to complete the task successfully? What did you notice when you received praise about your effort?

When I think of self-efficacy, learning mathematics comes to mind. Over a number of years of teaching, so many people believe they either can, or cannot do maths. Parents will sometimes tell me that their child is struggling with maths because they did as a child. They may also tell me that they cannot really help their child with any maths homework due to a lack of self-belief or self-confidence. When we hold the belief that we cannot do something, and have held this belief for many years, quite often we fulfil that belief, regardless of it being true or not. Henry Ford once said; "Whether you think that you can or you can't, you're usually right." Sandi remembers being told at primary school that she was no good at maths and recalls being in the 'bottom group', whatever that means. However, she is now a mathematical genius at home, balancing our family finances to the cent!

> "If I have the belief that I can do it, I shall surely acquire the capacity to do it even if I may not have it at the beginning."
>
> Mahatma Gandhi.

October Week 1

Independence

> "The greatest gifts you can give your children are the roots of responsibility and the wings of independence."
>
> Denis Waitley

Independence is having the ability to do something without help from others. It could be seen as the freedom of doing things on your own. Being independent can help us to increase our self-esteem and self-confidence. It may also make us more able to care for ourselves and others too. Being independent can help us to create our own destiny. However, being independent may mean that we sometimes don't ask for help from others. It may be limiting on our relationships with others. Many believe that being independent can help us reduce our stress levels and increase our happiness.

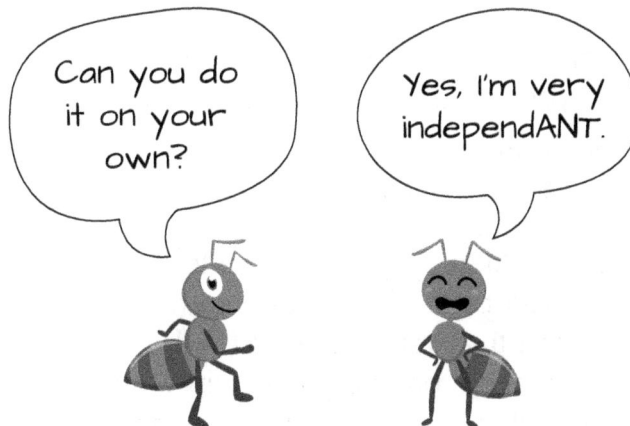

Choose one thing to try together from the following list to help foster independence at home. Have fun!

★ Play a quiz where each person takes turns to ask everyone else questions, like: What colour is the vacuum cleaner? Where is the hammer kept? How do you start the lawnmower? How do you put on a load of washing? What night do the bins go out? How do you use a bike pump?

★ Prepare and cook a healthy meal or snack for everyone else. Write a list of all the ingredients you need and also help purchase them.

★ What is an important skill you need to learn that will help you become more independent? Ask someone to help you learn this new skill.

★ Plan a weekend activity, picnic or family excursion.

★ What are the most important skills you need to learn before moving out of home? Rank them from most to least important to learn. Choose one of these skills and learn how to do it. How will you know when you have mastered this skill?

★ Think about some skills that you would like to learn, then go to YouTube and see if you can find a video that will teach you this new skill.

★ Arrange a play date with a friend. You will need to organise snacks and activities as well as how your friend will get to your place and travel home.

★ Open a bank account with some of your personal savings or some pocket money.

★ Tidy and reorganise your bedroom. Is there anything you don't need anymore that you could donate to the op shop?

★ Help with the shopping by writing a list, going to the market and when you get home, help to put it all away.

Often, when I'm teaching kids, they'll come up to me with issues or problems. I'm committed to children becoming independent learners and independent human beings. So, often the first thing that I will ask them is, "How are you going to sort that problem out on your own?" or, "Who are you going to ask to help you?" I have found that by asking questions in this way, I am letting them know that I believe that they are able to work things out on their own. I've found that children grow and become more independent when I give them many opportunities to experience independence. I also believe that if a child can do something for themselves, then they should do it.

"Independence is happiness."

Susan B. Anthony

October Week 2

Following Instructions

Following instructions could be defined as carrying out rules, requirements or guidelines. It is part of everyday life and starts early on. Following instructions is an important skill to enable us to function in a variety of environments. It may help us to achieve small goals and also to help us to survive. Imagine being caught in an emergency situation; sirens blaring and lights flashing. In race the police and fire fighters. They yell out some instructions and we have very little choice but to follow them or the outcome could be dire. We are all used to following instructions; however sometimes, our thoughts of what is said and what we think it may mean could be very different to what was actually said.

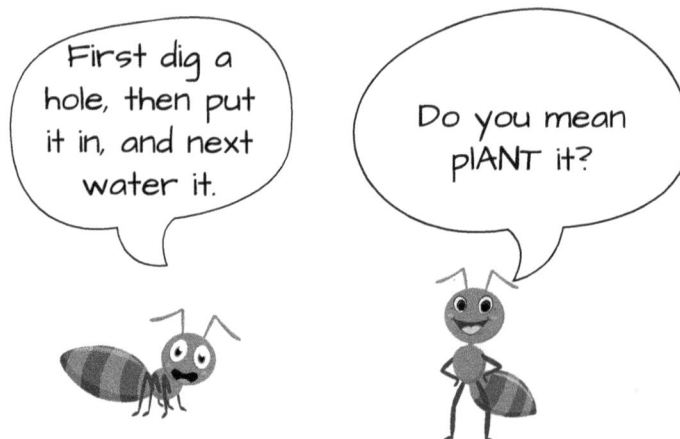

> First dig a hole, then put it in, and next water it.

> Do you mean plANT it?

Here is a list of ideas to try together to help foster the skill of following instructions.

★ Blindfold a partner and give verbal instructions to guide them around the house without touching them.

★ Teach each other to make a paper plane or an origami creation.

★ Play 'Simon Says' together as a family.

★ Cook something with a partner. One person gives all the instructions from the recipe and the other person must prepare and cook the dish.

★ One person acts as the boss and gives instructions to everyone else to clean the house.

★ Draw a simple picture, but do not show anyone else. Give others instructions on how to draw your picture without showing them. Whose picture was the closest? Repeat.

★ Have somebody teach everyone else in the family how to play a new game.

★ Get some blocks or Lego and work in a pair to build something together. One person gives the instructions and the other builds.

★ Make a scavenger hunt for everyone to complete. All instructions must be written down.

★ You must complete the following task as quickly as you can. Read all of the instructions below before doing anything, then start your timer and go.

1. Find a pen and paper.
2. Write your name at the top of the paper.
3. Write the numbers 1 to 5, one per line.
4. Draw five small circles beside #1.
5. Put an "X" in the second and fourth circles next to #1.
6. Write the word 'encyclopaedia' beside #3.
7. On the back of the paper multiply seven by nine.
8. Put an "X" in the lower right-hand corner of the paper.
9. Draw a circle around the "X" you just made.
10. Underline your name.

11. Say your name out aloud.
12. Draw a circle around #4.
13. Count the number of words in this sentence and write the answer beside #2 on your paper.
14. Put a square around #1 and #5.
15. Punch three small holes anywhere in the paper.
16. Write your first name beside #4.
17. Write today's date beside #5 on your paper.
18. Circle every letter "E" you have written.
19. Stand up and say 'I HAVE FINISHED FIRST', if you were first, or else say 'I HAVE FINISHED' out aloud, then sit down.
20. Now that you have read all of the instructions, skip all of them except the first two! If you have followed the instructions correctly, you should only have your name on the paper!

When I was young, I used to love making model aeroplanes and cars. The instructions could be quite complicated and it was often a slow process, as many parts needed to be painted and glued, and I would often have to wait for it to dry before moving on to the next stage. As an adult, my three kids have been given a lot of Lego and I've watched them build amazing constructions by following the instructions that contain no written words. I've noticed that kids of all ages seem to be able to naturally follow these instructions with very little help from anyone else. I've also loved watching them totally disregard the instructions and create some amazing things with their Lego. And the play that would follow the constructing would often last for days.

> "This planet came with a set of instructions, but we seem to have misplaced them. Civilization needs a new operating system."
>
> Paul Hawken

Negotiation

> "Relationships are a constant negotiation and balance."
>
> Claire Danes

Negotiation could usually involve some discussion aimed at reaching an agreement between two or more people. It may take some to-and-froing to settle where both are happy with the result. Negotiation is a useful skill to have in life as it can help us to resolve conflicts or solve problems. Children that have good negotiation skills may also become more independent, needing less help from an adult when faced with conflict. Good negotiators will need to be able to listen to others and be flexible. As Indian philosopher Maharishi Mahesh Yogi said, "To resolve problems through negotiation is a very childish approach."

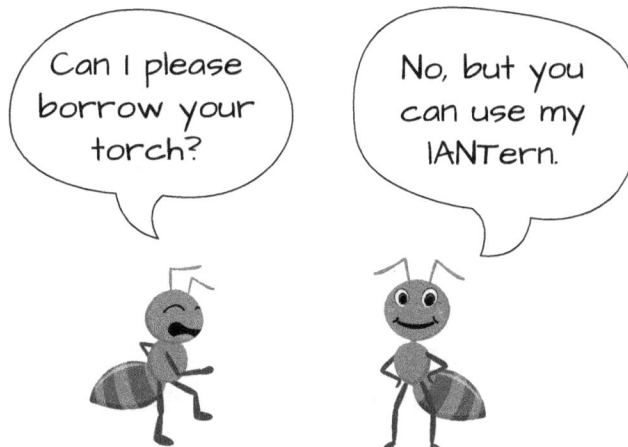

Can I please borrow your torch?

No, but you can use my lANTern.

Together as a family, discuss which activity you would like to do from the following list then negotiate until you all agree on which one to do this week.

★   Ask your partner to do something. Your partner needs to reply with, "I will do what you have asked once you have ..." Fill the gap. Discuss what you discovered.

★   Eat something really healthy. Then ask if you can eat something not so healthy, like this: "I've just eaten an apple and a pear. Could I please have a biscuit now?"

★   Do something kind for someone. Then ask if they will do something kind for you in return.

★   When you are asked to go to bed, ask if you can stay up for an extra 10 minutes if during that time, you give one of your parents a massage or a back tickle.

★   When you are having dinner, see if you can trade some food with someone else at the dinner table.

★   Play Monopoly together. Are there any other games you can play that involve negotiation?

★   Find a book that you have read before and see if you can trade it with a friend for a book that they have read.

★   Play a game where one person makes an offer to someone else. The person who receives the offer cannot say yes immediately, no matter how good the proposal may seem. See how much more you can negotiate for.

★   Go to the op shop or a garage sale and find something you like. Ask how much the item is then offer them a little less. See what happens.

★   When you are asked to do something, ask if you can do it in five minutes rather than straight away and see what happens.

I hear so many parents talk about the conflict within their family about time on electronic devices. With so many schools adopting a BYOD program (Bring Your Own Device), it seems to be increasingly difficult to avoid this equipment. But how would it be if the introduction of iPads into the home presented itself as an opportunity rather than a burden? Kids want more time on them while parents want less. Perhaps this could be an opportunity to connect through negotiation? My daughter, Daisy, loves to use her iPad to listen to music and she will often ask. Sometimes, I'll simply say yes. Sometimes, I'll ask her for how long and then we negotiate an agreeable time. And other times, I'll ask her what she can do first to help the family. She'll often offer to bring the washing in from the line and sort it all before spending time listening to music. Not only are we connecting with each other through a conversation without any conflict, Daisy is learning the important skill of negotiation. And, the washing has been brought in and sorted too!

> "There's no road map on how to raise a family:
> it's always an enormous negotiation."
>
> Meryl Streep

October Week 4

Disability Awareness

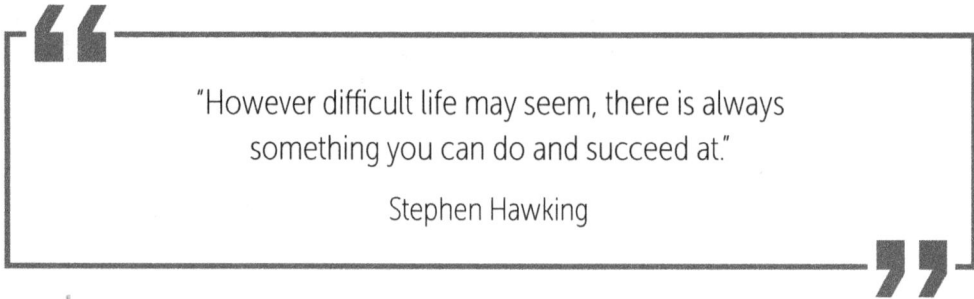

> "However difficult life may seem, there is always something you can do and succeed at."
>
> Stephen Hawking

Disability awareness is 'giving people the knowledge required to carry out a job or task, separating good practice from poor when communicating, working with or assisting a person with a disability' (www.disabilityawareness/net). Maybe it is treating a person with a disability as another equal human being with the same feelings and rights as someone without a disability. Having a knowledge of disability awareness may help to promote acceptance of people with a disability. It may also help us to all work together to foster positive attitudes within the community of people with a disability.

Following is a list of ideas to choose from to help learn about disability awareness. Choose your favourite and give it a go this week.

★ What do you think is the difference between tolerance and acceptance of someone with a disability? Discuss.

★ Discuss what you think are the differences between a physical disability and an intellectual disability.

★ If you met a person with a physical disability, what would you like to know if you could ask them anything? What about a person with an intellectual disability? Is there anything that you would like to find out if you could ask them anything?

★ Make a list of all the things that make you different from someone with a disability. Now make another list with all the things that you have that are the same.

★ If you could make some changes to your house, what could you do to make it more accessible to somebody with a physical disability?

★ Research some famous people with a disability. Discuss what is inspiring about them.

★ What would happen if a person with a disability joined your classroom or workplace? How could you make sure they were included with everyone else?

★ If you noticed that a car was in a disabled parking spot without a permit, could you do something to make a difference without upsetting anyone?

★ Research different disabilities and consider making a donation to help support a disability foundation.

★ Visit a hospital and ask them if you are able to try using a wheelchair. Talk about what you noticed.

My mum qualified as a teacher after finishing school and went on to study 'Special Education'. When I was growing up, she worked for many years at a school for children with special needs. Mum didn't see that those kids had special needs. Rather, she just saw them all as special. She saw all the kids she taught in regular state primary schools as special too. When she retired from teaching, Mum moved to Queensland. However, Mum had never really retired. She now works, caring for a severely disabled young adult called Rikky. A few times a week, Mum takes her for walks and a variety of different activities around their area. My mum is someone who sees people for who they are, regardless of the labels given to them or of their differences.

> "The world wasn't originally built for disabled people. Therefore, attitudes have been negatively affected too. Now disabled people have legislation for accessibility and inclusion, things are improving. Housing, transport, work, leisure and travel are all for the taking now. Political correctness has been the enemy of equality. Communication is the way."
>
> Martyn Sibley

November Week 1

Self-Confidence

> "With realisation of one's own potential and self-confidence in one's ability, one can build a better world."
>
> Dalai Lama

One thing that I believe helps to dramatically improve student results at school is self-confidence. If someone believes they can do something, more often than not, they will be able to do it. They may need some coaching or specific feedback; however, they are more likely to achieve their goals if they have self-confidence.

Self-confidence may be defined as having trust in oneself to be able to do something or to achieve a goal. Mastering a range of different skills may help us to build confidence in other areas of our lives. Self-confidence can help us develop our self-confidence even more.

When teaching, often children say that they aren't any good at something, say, reading, for example. Firstly, I'll ask them why they want to become a better reader. Then we talk about what they can do to help themselves. I let them know that I'll give them plenty of coaching and instruction, but they need to do their part. The other thing that I will do is connect them to some books that they enjoy. We'll visit the school library and local library and I'll help the kids to connect with books and experience the joy of reading. Their reading skills will naturally improve and so will their confidence with reading. I also notice that their self-confidence in other areas also lifts. When we are feeling confident, often we will take on challenges with the belief that we can achieve them.

Check out this list of ideas and choose one to try together to help boost self-confidence. Have fun!

★ What things have you achieved in the past few days, no matter how small they are? How has that made you feel?

★ Stand up, slump down and drop your shoulders. How does your body make you feel? Now make a pose like Superman. What is different now? Make some other poses that make you feel confident.

★ Do something really kind to someone. How did it make you feel?

★ Talk about some of the things that you love to do. Why are you good at them? How do you feel when you do them? How do you solve any problems you encounter when you are doing something you love?

★ Make a list of five things you are really good at. Which ones from your list would you be able to teach someone else to do?

★ Talk about things that you have been procrastinating from doing. Choose one thing to start doing tomorrow or on the weekend. What did you notice?

★ Go for a walk or bike ride and every time you pass someone, say, "Hi," and smile. What did you notice?

★ Help do a job or two around the house. Notice how it made you feel.

★ Dress up for dinner at home by wearing your favourite clothes and shoes. Do you feel any different?

★ Next time you are down the street or at the shops, start up a conversation with someone you don't know.

As a young child, Finn was never particularly physically coordinated and was fairly uninterested in sports. He often came close to last in any school sporting events and didn't really enjoy participating. He tried soccer, but didn't really like it too much. Finn tried tennis and things seemed to change. He got better and better. He had group lessons on Friday afternoons, which he loved. He had a couple of private lessons and his tennis improved even more. Sometimes, Finn would be given money for birthdays or Christmas and he'd often spend it on more tennis lessons. At the age of 12, Finn plays in tennis tournaments and practises with a group of adults from the local tennis club on Wednesday nights. Finn's self-confidence with his sport has increased tenfold in the last few years. He now even enjoys running at school sports events.

> "Doing projects really gives people self-confidence. Nothing is better than taking the pie out of the oven. What it does for you personally, and for your family's idea of you, is something you can't buy."
>
> Martha Stewart

Integrity

> "With integrity, you have nothing to fear, since you have nothing to hide. With integrity, you will do the right thing, so you will have no guilt."
>
> Zig Ziglar

Many dictionary definitions of integrity seem to say the same two things. Firstly, it is having the quality of honesty and secondly, having strong moral principles. Another definition I've heard is that integrity is simply keeping your word. Some believe it is doing the 'right' thing, whatever that is. Oprah Winfrey was quoted as saying 'real integrity is doing the right thing, knowing that nobody's going to know whether you did it or not'.

When we have integrity, we may experience feelings of peace and we may feel good within ourselves. Having integrity helps us to stand out above others. We also do what we say we'll do and do it on time. And, if we can't keep our word, we will be responsible for not doing so. Integrity can be a powerful attribute as we become known as people who keep our word and always do what others would expect us to do.

Here are a few ideas to help foster the skill of integrity. Choose the one that best fits your family and try it this week.

★ Name some people you know that have integrity. What are those people like? What is important about integrity? Discuss.

★ Play a board game or card game and cheat just a little bit so you don't get caught. How did you feel just before you cheated? What about later on in the game or at the end of it?

★ Have you ever found anything that was not yours and you really wanted to keep it? Did you keep it or try and find the owner? How did you feel if you found the owner? How did you feel if you kept it?

★ Go for a walk and say you will be back by a certain time. Make sure you arrive home a little bit later than you said you would. Make a list of excuses as to why you were late. What is the difference between being on time, and being late with an excuse? Discuss.

★ If you give your word and say you will do something, what happens if you cannot keep your word? Can you have integrity if you do not keep your word? Think of some situations where you may not have been able to keep your word. Discuss.

★ Play 'Two Truths and a Lie' where you say two things that are true about yourself and one thing that is not. The others must guess which the lie is.

★ Sometime during the week when you are asked something, respond with a lie. How did you feel? How long did you take to own up and tell the truth?

★ Request that someone in your family do something for you by a certain time. If they accept, see if they do exactly what you requested by the time your requested it. What did you both notice?

★ Do you think that someone can always be in integrity? What happens if someone promises to do something and they don't do it? How can they restore their integrity? Is simply apologising enough?

★ Sneak something from the pantry that you are not normally allowed to eat. What did you notice and how did you feel? Did you eventually own up?

When I was in high school, I was visiting some friends and we decided to play some basketball in the street. I threw the ball and it hit a car, breaking the wing mirror on the front door. I felt terrible, so I wrote my name, address and phone number on a piece of paper with an explanation of what had happened. I received a phone call a few days later and told the owner of the car that I knew a panel beater who could fix his mirror. My friend fixed it at a reduced cost to me, to which I was extremely thankful. The guy who owned the car was also very thankful for my honesty. Even though I was out of pocket a fair bit of money for a teenager, I knew that I remained in integrity.

> "The supreme quality for leadership is unquestionably integrity. Without it, no real success is possible, no matter whether it is on a section gang, a football field, in an army, or in an office."
>
> Dwight D. Eisenhower

I always do what I say I'll do.

I can constANTly rely on you to keep your word.

Mindfulness

> "You practice mindfulness, on the one hand, to be calm and peaceful. On the other hand, as you practice mindfulness and live a life of peace, you inspire hope for a future of peace."
>
> Thich Nhat Hanh

Mindfulness could be thought of as a calm and focused effort to be present to the moment. It could be an awareness of our thoughts, feelings, bodily sensations, and surrounding environment without judgement. Mindfulness is not thinking about the past or the future. Some scientists believe that practising mindfulness can help us reduce our anxiety and help us avoid depression. They also say that it can reduce our distractions and improve focus. American author, scientist and mindfulness expert, Jon Kabat-Zinn, said, "In Asian languages, the word for 'mind' and the word for 'heart' are same. So, if you're not hearing mindfulness in some deep way as heartfulness, you're not really understanding it. Compassion and kindness towards oneself are intrinsically woven into it. You could think of mindfulness as wise and affectionate attention."

Mindfulness might also be thought of as being in the moment, or being present to what is happening right now. 'If you are depressed you are living in the past. If you are anxious you are living in the future. If you are at peace you are living in the present.' Lao Tsu

To help foster mindfulness, choose your favourite from the following list to do together as a family this week.

★ As a family, do some colouring in together in silence. Listen to the noises outside. Can you hear the pencils rubbing on the paper? What other noises do you notice? What body sensations do you feel?

★ Turn off the lights and sit quietly somewhere. Notice your breathing. Feel each breath as it enters your body and then calmly exits. Do this for five or 10 minutes. Talk about what you noticed.

★ Go for a walk to the local park, river or beach. Sit quietly and listen to the sounds around you. Take some paper and a pencil and divide your page into five parts. In each section, write down everything you hear, what you see, any smells you notice, anything you physically feel and also the emotions that you feel.

★ At night time, turn off all the lights and put on some relaxing music and listen.

★ When you are having a meal together, choose one item of food from your plate. Look carefully at it before smelling it then slowly eating it. Talk about all the things that you notice before doing it again with another item of food.

★ Blindfold someone in the group. Have them smell different items and let them describe what they smell. Does the smell remind them of anything else? Repeat with taste, touch and listening.

★ Exercise vigorously for a minute. Sit quietly and notice all the different sensations in your body. After discussing what you all noticed, sit quietly for a minute and then discuss what is different. Finally, exercise vigorously for another minute and see if you notice anything different from the first time.

★ Download the free app 'Smiling Mind' and have a play with it. See what you discover.

★ Go outside and lie on the grass and watch the clouds float past. Try this during the day and also when it starts to get dark at night.

★ When you are brushing your teeth, notice all the sensations in your mouth. What do you taste? Can you smell anything? Focus on the movement of the toothbrush in your mouth. Discuss what you noticed with everyone else.

Recently, with my Grade One students, I've started to teach and practise mindfulness. First, I let them quietly colour in different sheets. Next, they use textas to scribble with flowing lines before they coloured the spaces they had made. They really enjoyed the colouring and chatting to each other. What I discovered was they appeared to be more mindful when I was directing their thoughts. I would be calmly talking and putting them in touch with the current moment they were in by saying things like, "Gently feel your feet touching the floor through your shoes. Notice if the carpet feels soft or fluffy. Wriggle your toes in your shoes and notice which toe moves more. As you are colouring, quietly listen to the noise your pencil makes as it rubs on the paper. Notice how the pencil feels in your hand. Is it smooth or is it hard? Can you listen carefully to the sounds outside?" What I noticed was the children were more present to the moment and there was a very calm and relaxed mood in the room.

> "Mindfulness is about love and loving life. When you cultivate this love, it gives you clarity and compassion for life, and your actions happen in accordance with that."
>
> Jon Kabat-Zinn

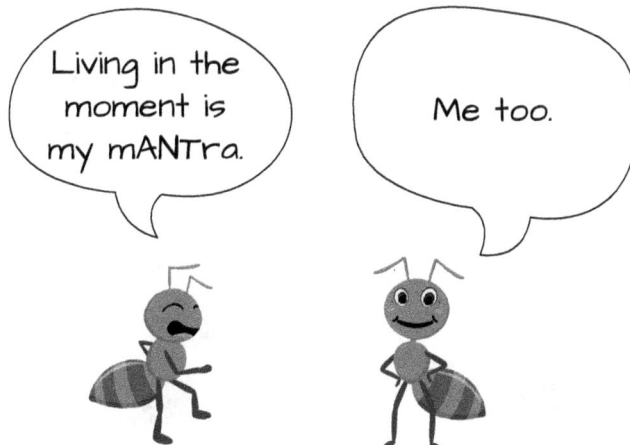

Living in the moment is my mANTra.

Me too.

Fun

> "Just play. Have fun. Enjoy the game."
> Michael Jordan

Fun, entertainment, amusement, pleasure, enjoyment or excitement. Who doesn't want more of this in their lives? Actor Nina Dobrev said, "Even though you're growing up, you should never stop having fun." Maybe a clown doesn't need more fun, but I'm not really sure. There are many health benefits for us all for having fun. Many fun scientists have proven that it helps us to reduce stress and improve our ability to cope. I believe that it can help to improve concentration and memory, and other things that I can't really remember. Fun can also help us to create more energy. Fun, fun, fun.

Nothing like a good giggle eh?

And some old fashioned bANTer too.

Check out this list and choose one from it to help you all have some fun together this week.

- ★ Make a list of some fun things you all like to do together as a family. Plan to do some of them this week, some this month and some later on.

- ★ Google 'fun things to do in your area' or 'fun things to do at home'. Pick the top few that you all agree on and do some of them.

- ★ Choose some card games or board games that you all love to play together.

- ★ What does fun mean to you? Do others agree or disagree with you? What is the opposite of fun for you?

- ★ Organise a picnic or barbeque at the local park with your family. You might like to invite some other friends along too. Plan some fun games and activities to do while you are there.

- ★ Plan a fun family movie night. Once you have chosen your film, don't forget the snacks.

- ★ Play Charades or Celebrity Heads together as a family.

- ★ Read some children's picture storybooks together.

- ★ Make a list of your favourite fun activities you like to do and plan to do some of them with your friends.

- ★ Talk about all the fun things you did today. What about yesterday? What did you do that was fun lately? Talk about all the fun things you love to do.

I asked everyone in the family who their friends are that are most fun to be with. We all talked about their different friends and what they like to do with them. But why is it important to have fun with them was my next question. We all discussed that we liked to laugh and live in the moment with our friends. Daisy said that she liked to live in the moment. When I ask my kids in the classroom why they like to do certain things, they will often respond with "because it's fun". My brother, Tim, has always made his life fun. He is a passionate Australian football supporter and he loves motor racing. In the past few years, Tim has found another passion and started a business promoting health with raw and fermented foods. Earlier on in his working life, he could never keep a job or do anything that wasn't fun. Tim is one person who seems to have so much fun with his life.

> "At the end of the day, if I can say I had fun, it was a good day."
>
> Simone Biles

December Week 1

Being You

Being you? What does that really mean? Aren't you just you anyway? Maybe we are just who we are. Or, maybe sometimes we aren't really ourselves; perhaps we aren't always being true to ourselves.

I know I've been in many situations where I've just gone along with the crowd, agreed with others so I fit in. I have also stayed away from 'sticky' situations so I don't upset others. However, sometimes I'm not really being me. As a child, I found this more difficult to be true to myself as I was often concerned about 'looking good'. However, as I grow older, I find that I'm less concerned with how others may think of me.

Maybe this is great to be more comfortable with who I am and what I believe. However, maybe this isn't so good, as others may think that I have no concern for how they feel. Sounds like another one of those conundrums where I'm not sure what is right and what is wrong. Sounds like life, I reckon.

Some of the benefits of being ourselves could be that we are more honest with who we are and what is important to us. We may find that we are in integrity, being true to ourselves even if it may not be the easy or comfortable thing to do. Being ourselves may help us lead a life with less regrets too. As we get older, I wonder if we all become less concerned with how we look?

Here are a few ideas to help encourage you to be you. Choose one from the list and try it this week with your family.

★ What makes you special? Write a list of all the things that make you different from everyone else. Compare your list to others in your family. Can you add anything to another person's list?

★ Go to the mirror and have a good look at your face. Look at your nose, your eyes, your ears and your chin. Now look at your teeth and skin. Take note of any distinctive marks on your face. Can you notice any small marks? See how long you can look at yourself in the mirror. Once everyone else has done this, discuss what you noticed.

★ Talk about some of the things that you have failed at. What did you learn about yourself when you made these failures?

★ Do you know anyone that is really happy with who they are? Why do you think they are so happy? What is it that you admire about them?

★ Talk about some of your funny habits. Does anyone else in your family have a similar habit? What about anyone else you know?

★ Have someone say something they notice about you. Your job is to respond with, "It's just the way I am, and that's okay."

★ What do you dream that you could do if nothing stopped you? Talk together about all your dreams for an amazing life.

★ Lao Tzu said, "At the centre of your being you have the answer; you know who you are and you know what you want." What does this mean to you? Discuss.

★ Make a list of some important things you have already achieved in your life. Why are they important to you?

★ Now make a new list of all the things that you wish to achieve in your life. Which ones are really important and which are not so important? Put them in order from most to least important.

One of the great things about working with young children is that they often really don't care about what anyone else thinks about them. They are just themselves. Being a parent has given me the joy of spending time with my children and seeing them just be themselves. Daisy was always creative from a young child. She would draw, paint, make and play. As she grows older, Daisy continues to be creative with her music, art and creations in the kitchen. Finn was always a happy kid, who loved to play and as he is getting older, he is still playing. Instead of playing with toys and cars, Finn plays tennis. From the day Monty was born, he has always enjoyed a laugh and that's the way Monty still is. He loves any form of comedy and is often laughing and playing with his friends. I hope that my three children continue to stay true to themselves, and follow their dreams and continue to create amazing lives for themselves.

> "Here's to the crazy ones. The misfits. The rebels. The troublemakers. The round pegs in the square holes. The ones who see things differently. They're not fond of rules. And they have no respect for the status quo. You can quote them, disagree with them, glorify or vilify them. About the only thing you can't do is ignore them. Because they change things. They push the human race forward. And while some may see them as the crazy ones, we see genius. Because the people who are crazy enough to think they can change the world, are the ones who do."
>
> Steve Jobs

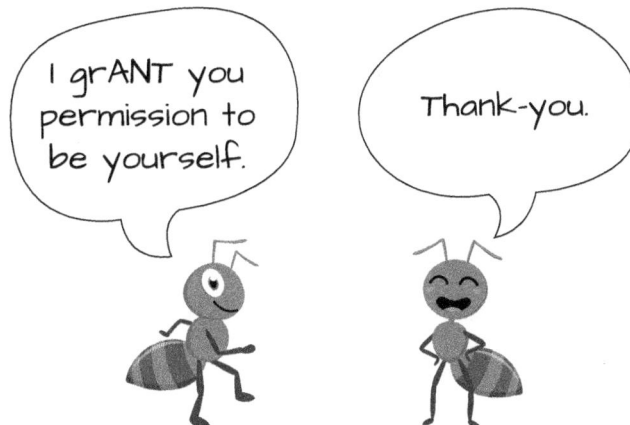

Perseverance

> "Perseverance is the hard work you do after you get tired of doing the hard work you already did."
>
> Newt Gingrich

'Never give up' might be a good fit to describe perseverance. Even when things become challenging or difficult, persevering can help us achieve our goals. Perseverance can sometimes be linked to endurance athletes or athletes with a disability. They often work extremely long hours during often difficult conditions to get to the top of their chosen sport. Perseverance is an attribute that could help us when taking on new challenges, particularly when things become difficult and we want to give up, which may be an acceptable thing to do for most people.

However, pushing through when the going gets tough moves us to a different place where we may often look back after the new learning has been acquired and wonder why we thought that task was so challenging. For me, being inactive and sitting at a desk for long periods of time is challenging. However, I break the large tasks into smaller, more manageable chunks and do small bits at a time, eventually completing the larger task. Before I even get started, I'll work out what is required then make a list of all the things I need to do before writing a list and assigning a date to complete each smaller part. That way, I'll persevere and complete a goal I set out to. Persevering at tasks may help us achieve our goals.

Here are some things that might help you become better at persevering. Choose your favourite from the list and try it this week.

- ★ Make a paper plane and have a competition to see whose plane can travel 10 metres. If your plane doesn't make the distance, try another design until it does.

- ★ Discuss some things that you aim to achieve no matter what. Will there be any hurdles you may encounter along the way? How will you overcome them?

- ★ Think of a time that you worked really hard to get something done. How did you overcome any challenges? How did you feel when you finally achieved your goal?

- ★ Build a really big house of cards. If it falls down, start again. How many decks of cards can you include in your construction?

- ★ Choose a part of your garden that needs weeding or maintenance. Start working in the garden and don't stop until you have finished.

- ★ Learn to cook a meal that you have never made before. Prepare and cook it for the family.

- ★ Think about a sport that you enjoy playing. Set up a difficult challenge and aim to achieve it. How long did it take you? Did you feel like giving up?

- ★ Make a list of a few tasks that you would like to achieve this week. Put them in order of what you would like to achieve first, second, third and so on. Then break each task into small parts and list them. Each time you achieve each small part, tick it off before going on to the next small part. What did you notice about ticking off each part as you went? Did you achieve all your tasks this week?

- ★ Start to tidy your bedroom or a cupboard in the house and don't stop until it is totally complete.

- ★ Plan a long family walk or bike ride together that you know will be challenging. Commit to completing the walk or ride no matter what. How did you all feel when you finished?

I've always ridden a bike. I love bikes and I love riding them. I always have. Over 10 years ago, I met someone called Nev. He invited me to join him on an early morning bike ride for a distance of about 20 kilometres. After some time, more and more people joined us on regular morning rides. We started to ride every weekday morning for about an hour. The group organised a few longer weekend rides. More cyclists joined in. One morning over a post-ride coffee, Mikey suggested that we all ride from the Sydney Harbour Bridge to our home town's Barwon Heads Bridge. Hence, the B2B was born – Bridge to Bridge. We trained for over a year; some more than others. There was a range of ages, fitness levels and abilities. When it came to April of 2016, we started our ride from Sydney, south along the coast. We all rode as a team, supporting each other through rain, wind and even sunshine. We cycled up some huge hills and raced down them. Together, we all managed to keep on going until we reached our destination eight days later in Barwon Heads.

> "Perseverance, secret of all triumphs."
> Victor Hugo

I never give up.

You are very persistANT.

December Week 3

Stress Management

> "You need to be able to manage stress because hard times will come, and a positive outlook is what gets you through."
>
> Marie Osmond

Stress could be defined as something that causes the body to become tense in some way. Being able to manage stress or situations that may cause us to become stressed could be a positive attribute. Many scientists believe that reducing stress can help to improve both physical and mental health. They also think that it can help to prolong life. Stress has been linked to anxiety and depression. It has been said that stress can even contribute to making you cranky! Who would have thought?

Managing our stress levels helps us to create a calm environment around us; a place where others may like to be. Managing stress may also help us get more

I'm feeling really frANTic.

Relax dude.

done by keeping a clear and focused direction. We may find that not only do we get more done, but we are able to create more time to do other things that we may really enjoy.

Choose your favourite from the following list to try together at home to help learn to manage your stress levels.

- ★ Make a list of all the things you need to do. Next, put them in order from most to least important. Now, just do the first thing on the top of your list. How did you feel when you completed just one thing?

- ★ Try some simple meditation together. You may wish to search YouTube or Google.

- ★ Find a good place to sit away from any distractions and close your eyes. Listen to the sounds around you. Focus on your feet and how they feel. Slowly, work your way up your body, noticing how each part of your body is feeling. What smells can you notice?

- ★ Tell each other jokes that you know or borrow a joke book from the library. Were any of the jokes funny? What did you notice when you heard a really funny joke?

- ★ Have someone in your family give you a back or foot tickle, or a gentle shoulder massage. How did it make you feel?

- ★ Go for a family walk together around the neighbourhood or to the local park. Consider watching the sunset together.

- ★ Do some yoga together as a family. Try searching on YouTube for some basic yoga sessions.

- ★ Play a board game or card game together.

- ★ Download a free meditation app, such as 'Smiling Mind', and see what you discover.

- ★ Go to the local pool, river or beach and have a swim.

A few years ago, as our kids started to get older, we started to look at how we could create more room for our family. We could sell and move to a larger house, but we really loved our home. After a lot of conversations and a few years, we decided to convert the garage into a separate studio and build a new garage onto the end of the house in the space that was always poorly used. Eventually, we came up with final plans and had them passed through Council. I decided to manage the extension on my own by being an 'owner builder'.

The first step was to build the new garage. Once complete, we then converted the old double garage into a studio space with a small bathroom, bedroom, loft and larger open lounge space. This took a lot of organisation; meeting with the various tradesmen, understanding the plans and ordering and coordinating delivery of building materials. The whole project took about a year, all while working fulltime. Once complete, the extra living space was tremendous, particularly when guests came to stay.

However, over time, we realised that we weren't really using the new studio as much as we wanted. We asked Daisy if she would like to move out to the studio, which would give the kids a room each. However, Daisy didn't want to move as she felt she'd be too disconnected from the family. On a weekend away, Sandi and I discussed this issue and we hatched a plan to knock a hole in the wall at the end of the hallway to connect the main house through to the studio.

Once again, plans, meetings with tradesmen, ordering and coordinating the delivery of building materials, all while I was working fulltime. A few months later, with the building works complete, we moved our master bedroom into the studio and now have a house just the right size for us.

Looking back, at times it could have been a lot more stressful than it was. However, by being organised and knowing the processes and different steps to take, the overall building process ran fairly smoothly and stress-free.

> "
> "Being in control of your life and having realistic expectations about your day-to-day challenges are the keys to stress management, which is perhaps the most important ingredient to living a happy, healthy and rewarding life."
>
> Marilu Henner.
> "

December Week 4

Love

> "There is only one happiness in this life, to love and be loved."
>
> George Sand

As Trinidadian-German singer, Haddaway, asked in his 1993 hit, "What is love?" So, what is love? There are many dictionary definitions and explanations from various philosophers over time. Some say it is a tender affection or personal attachment towards another. There are many benefits of experiencing love, such as improved connection with others and better physical and mental health. It may even help us have a longer and happier life. Some say that love can help reduce stress and feel more upbeat.

Whatever love is, the Dalai Lama seemed to sum it up best when he said, "Love and compassion are necessities, not luxuries. Without them humanity cannot survive."

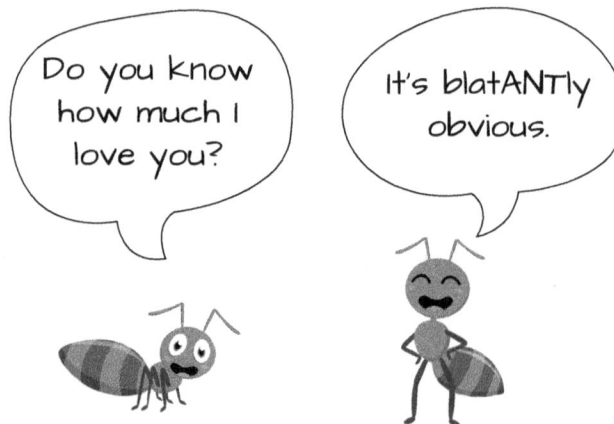

Choose something from the following list to help create even more love in your family. Enjoy!

- ★ Draw a big love heart and inside it, list of all the people that you love and the people who love you.

- ★ Think about someone you love and perform a random act of kindness for them. Repeat.

- ★ Go on a special parent-child date together. Only one parent and one child.

- ★ Write everyone's name in the family onto a separate piece of paper. Write one thing you love about each person. Put all the notes into a jar then read them out one at a time.

- ★ Make a card for someone you love. Inside the card, just tell them that you love them then give it to them.

- ★ Write a list of some things that you enjoy doing together as a family and see how many of them you can do.

- ★ Send someone a Valentine's Day card even if it isn't Valentine's Day.

- ★ What does unconditional love mean to you? Discuss.

- ★ The Dali Lama said that "Love and compassion are necessities..." What do you think? Discuss.

- ★ Find someone you love and give them a really big hug. Repeat many times.

I feel so blessed to have the family that we have created. How different life would have been if I did not meet Sandi in London all those years ago. I love Sandi so much and also love our three kids, Daisy, Finn and Monty. No matter what choices they make in their lives, I know that I'll always love them so much. They are all such amazing people and it is such a pleasure to be a part of their lives and watch them grow.

I also feel so much love to my parents, Rob and Kate. Although they separated many years ago, they are the reason that I have been given a life. I remember thanking them for giving me life many years ago and I am still so grateful for them both for creating me, helping me to grow and being with me whenever I have needed them.

I have also been blessed with my siblings that I truly love. We often go for long periods of time without communicating with each other; however, I know that does not affect my love for them. Then there is Sandi's family, whom I am also grateful for and whom I also love. And there have been so many friends throughout my journey so far, whom I have loved along the way. Love – I'm not sure what the world would be like without it. And I wonder what the world could be like if there was only love.

> "Being deeply loved by someone gives you strength, while loving someone deeply gives you courage."
>
> Lao Tzu

Acknowledgements

This book is offered as a humble gesture of love for my wife Sandi, our children Daisy, Finn and Monty, and my parents Kate and Rob.

There are many people who have contributed to this book in countless ways. I thank my dad for all the feedback and numerous conversations in developing ideas for this book. Thanks to Nick for his creative photography, Jeanne, Sally and Sandi for their editing, and Sylvie for putting it all together. Also, thanks to Julian, Ian, Bec and Darryl who have supported me through the process of running the workshops as I began this project. I would also like to acknowledge the support from the families of Ocean Grove and Barwon Heads, who have attended the workshops and contributed in so many ways. Finally, I would like to thank Sandi, Daisy, Finn and Monty for inspiring me to write this book.

Without the support and encouragement of family, friends and colleagues, I could not have written this book. I am truly grateful.

Andy McNeilly